Celtic Cross Stitch Designs

Carol Phillipson

Guild of Master Craftsman Publications

First published in 1999 by
Guild of Master Craftsman Publications Ltd,
166 High Street, Lewes,
East Sussex BN7 1XU

Reprinted 2000

ISBN 1 86108 144 8

Cover photographer: Anthony Bailey
Cover designer: Rob Wheele at Wheelhouse Design
Photographer: Christine Richardson
Designer: Fineline Studios
Typefaces: Connach and Cochin
Colour separation: Viscan Graphics (Singapore)
Printed and bound: Printed in Great Britain at the
University Press, Cambridge

Dedication

I would like to give a very special mention
to my husband Alan without whose help,
enthusiasm and support this book would
not have been completed.

Acknowledgements

I would like to thank Catherine Phillipson
and Lorraine Wise for their help in
stitching some of the designs. Special
thanks go to Ann Hebb, not only for her
stitching, but also her enthusiasm and
support.
I am grateful to Fabric Flair Limited for
providing all of the fabrics and coasters, to
Coats Crafts UK for supplying all of the
threads and to Framecraft Miniatures for
the pots and other accessories from their
range. I must also thank Impress Cards and
Crafts who supplied cards, and Macgregor
Designs for their fine wooden footstool and
pincushion.

The publishers would like to thank
Jevoncraft, Lewes, for supplying tools and
materials featured in the photographs.

CONTENTS

About the author

Carol was born in Scarborough, North Yorkshire, but has lived in the East Riding of Yorkshire for many years with her husband Alan and two daughters. She trained as a teacher, and still teaches part-time in her village school. She has always been interested in embroidery and design, and with a friend started a needlework kit business. This has now been sold, and for the last ten years Carol has been a freelance needlework designer, working mainly for magazines and kit companies.

She spends a lot of time walking in the Derbyshire Dales, but some form of embroidery is always at hand. Carol thinks that one of the nicest things about stitching is that it is so portable and can be done almost anywhere.

Introduction

When I first undertook to write this book, as a designer, not an historian, my initial ideas centred on knots, plaits and borders, the most commonly found designs. However, when I began to research the designs used by the Celts, a myriad of stitching ideas opened up before me. Not only were there the beautifully decorated manuscripts such as the *Book of Kells* and the *Lindisfarne Gospels*, but also there were all the designs found on the jewellery and metal artefacts such as scabbards, weapons, torques, pottery, bronze and horse trappings, as well as all the carvings on stone.

Considering that many of these were made in the 6th and 7th centuries, it was surprising to me to find such a wealth of material still in existence. As I was writing one single book and not the first volume in a series, I had to sift and sort out ideas to provide an exciting, yet practical, set of designs which would inspire both beginners and experienced stitchers.

All of the designs in the book are taken from, or inspired by, the Celts. In many cases I have combined several ideas together to create the finished needlework. The book contains over one hundred design ideas, and as you can adapt these using the wide colour range of stranded cotton, tapestry wools and specialist threads now available, endless stitching projects are possible, limited perhaps only by time. It is surprising how stitching time seems to expand, perhaps at the expense of sleep!

I hope you derive as much excitement and pleasure from using these designs as I have had preparing them, and perhaps, like me, you may become sufficiently curious to discover more about the life of these people who lived over 1,200 years ago and are such an important part of our heritage.

Materials, Equipment and Stitches

The basic tools to enable you to stitch any (or all!) of the designs in this book are simple. I have used fabrics and threads that are all readily available, and have included many small designs to use up odd pieces of fabric and remaining threads.

General Accessories

Scissors are important. I have two pairs of needlework scissors; a small, sharp, pointed pair, and a large pair. The small ones are only to be used for threads and I have even fastened a piece of wool on the handle to remind the rest of the family! I use the larger ones for cutting canvas, fabric and Vilene. I never use either of these for cutting paper, as this is notorious for blunting even the sharpest scissors.

The most useful item that I have recently acquired is a small pair of round magnets which fit on either side of the fabric that is being stitched and trap the chart so that it stays in view at the edge of the embroidery frame. They also make a safe place to leave a needle. These are certainly invaluable.

A good light is a wise investment. There are many that are specifically designed for embroiderers, but I find a good, well-placed spotlight equally acceptable.

Blunt-ended needles should always be used for counted-thread work because they don't split the threads and weaken them. I find a size 22 or 24 ideal for evenweave and size 18 for canvas-work.

Fabric

For each item in the book the fabric actually used is stated, but a substitute can often be used. Where a substitution may not work, I have given the exact name. All of the fabrics in the book were supplied by Fabric Flair Limited. I have used mainly Aida, Jobelan and canvas. Aida is the easiest to use, but many stitchers, including myself, prefer to work over 2 threads on Jobelan. If you are substituting a different fabric, remember that the higher the thread count, the finer the stitching becomes.

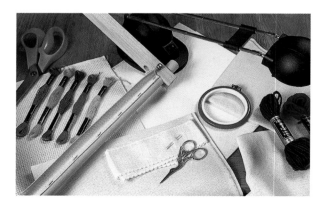

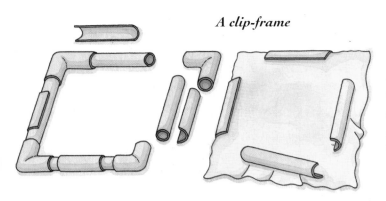
A clip-frame

Stitches

Although the book is called *Celtic Cross Stitch Designs*, I have included half-cross stitch and tent stitch to give variation. Tent stitch gives a better, denser covering than half-cross stitch and is more durable for items that will be subjected to a lot of wear.

Threads

The majority of the projects in the book are in either stranded cotton or tapestry wool, but I have included some variations, either for the colouring or texture. I find the wide range of threads and colours available a never-ending source of inspiration.

Frames

The use and type of frames is a personal matter. Some stitchers never use one, whilst others always do. Although it is tempting sometimes not to bother, I am one of the people who always uses one, because I find the end result more pleasing. It certainly minimizes the need for stretching and adjusting.

Although I have a number of different frames, I really only use three. All my canvas-work and large projects are now done on a clip-frame. These are a recent development and comprise a collection of light-weight plastic tubes and clips that can be made into a variety of sizes. The fabric is simply laid over the frame and tensioners are placed over to keep it in place. A simple twist adjusts the tension. They really have taken the hard work out of putting fabric on a frame and, moreover, they don't damage or mark the fabric. For smaller evenweave designs I use a hoop frame, either a wooden seat frame, which leaves both hands free for stitching, or a plastic flexi-hoop for very small items.

Half-cross stitch

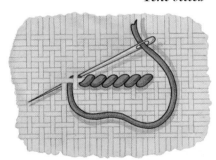
Tent stitch

CROSS STITCH

First leg of cross stitch

Completion of cross stitch

Adapting the Designs

While writing this book, one of my main aims was to give every reader a 'library' of Celtic patterns to be used wherever they are needed. The stitched pieces have been made up into various objects and the details of the charts, thread colours, thread counts and fabrics used have been given. I have tried to demonstrate different ideas to be used in your own stitched projects. If you are changing things around and experimenting, it is important to plan carefully before you start stitching.

Nothing could be worse than the design disappearing off the side of the fabric because it isn't wide enough! Charted designs can be worked on any fabric with even threads. The number given to evenweave fabrics, e.g. 14#, means that there are 14 threads to 1in (2.5cm) and therefore, if you are working over every thread, you will stitch 14 stitches for every inch. Similarly, if you work on 28# fabric, but work over 2 threads, which happens quite often in the book, you are still working 14 stitches in one inch. Stitching a design on a fabric with fewer threads to one inch will enlarge the stitching, but you may then need an extra strand of cotton to cover the canvas or fabric. Always try stitching a small sample and adjust it before starting the main project. Conversely, if the thread count is greater, the work will be smaller and may need less thread.

One obvious example of this is in the knot section. The same chart, when worked in wool on 10# canvas is suitable for a rug, in two strands of cotton on 14# is suitable for a cushion, and on 22# canvas it makes a small picture. In the latter case the number of strands has been increased in order to cover the canvas.

To calculate the size of a stitched piece, take the stitch count and divide it by the number of threads per inch of the fabric. For example, take a design with 22 squares. This will cover 1in (2.5cm) when stitched on 22# (22 divided by 22). It will cover just under 1¼in (3.1cm) when stitched on 18# (18 divided by 22), 1⁹⁄₁₆in (4cm) on 14# (14 divided by 22), and 2³⁄₁₆in (5.6cm) when stitched on 10# (10 divided by 22).

Other ways of making the stitching fit a larger frame include adding a border or a card mount.

Colours are a personal choice. These colours are my choice, but may not be yours. Don't be afraid of changing them. It will usually be more successful if you try to keep to the darker tones in my design. You can see below how the bedding border changes when the colours are changed in the design.

Altering the type of thread, for example adding some metallic gold, soft cotton or

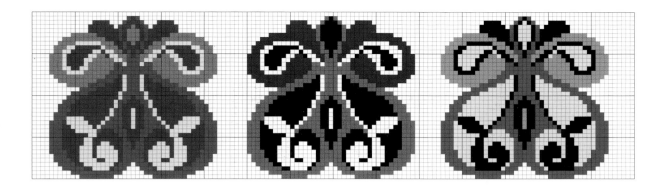

perle thread, gives a different texture. You do need to bear in mind the amount of wear the article will receive. For instance, using gold metallic thread in a picture or pot lid would be fine, but it would soon wear out if used in a rug that was being walked on constantly.

One of my favourite parts of designing is adding the finishing touches. A few beads, a tassel, a twisted cord or a lace-edging costs very little, and doesn't take long to do, but it can make a great deal of difference to the completed stitching.

Making a tassel

Take a piece of card slightly longer than your tassel is to be. Wrap thread round the card until it is fairly thick. Loop a piece of

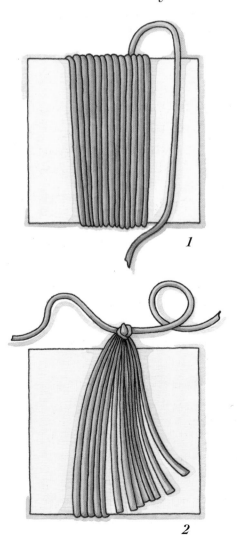

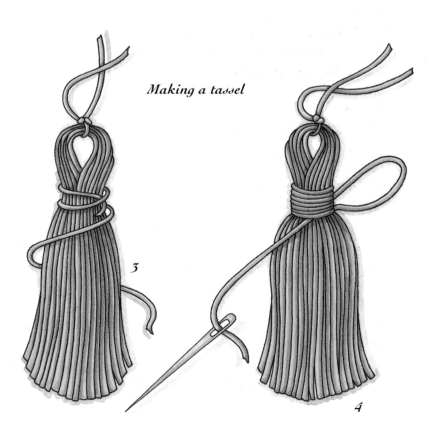

Making a tassel

thread between the card and the wound threads at the top, pull it tight and knot it. Then cut the threads from the card at the bottom. Smooth the threads down and tightly wind a new length of thread to form a tassel. Using a needle, thread the end down so that the secured end becomes part of the tassel. Use the thread at the top to fasten the tassel to the stitching.

Making a twisted cord

First decide how long the cord needs to be. Always make it a bit longer than you really want it, because it is easy to trim. I cut the threads three times the required length of the cord, and half as thick as I would like it to be. Fasten a knot at both ends then thread one end over a door handle and thread a pencil through the other. Keeping it fairly tight twist, the pencil round and round the same way until it is tightly twisted. Take hold of the twisted thread in the centre and put the two ends together. The cord will automatically twist on itself. Remember to keep it taut as you bring the ends together, then it will twist evenly.

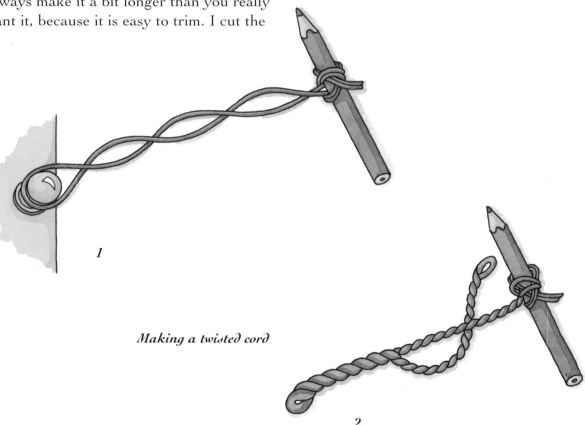

Making a twisted cord

1

2

The Designs

MACHINES ON THE MOON

Machines for use on the Moon have interested men of science through the centuries but the need for practical machines became a reality after the first Moon landing in 1969. However, both the Russians and the Americans had already achieved much in this field in the early parts of their space programmes. The space agencies of both countries launched various probes which made soft landings on the Moon. The American *Surveyor* series sent back pictures of the Moon's surface and one of the later Russian probes, *Luna 16,* scooped up a sample of soil and sent it safely back to Earth. The first wheeled vehicle to land and explore the Moon was the Russian *Lunokhod 1*, but perhaps the most well-known machine was the American Moon Rover which was part of the equipment used by the Apollo 15 astronauts.

SIMON SNORKEL SS 85. This vehicle has a hydrauli-
cally-operated mobile aerial platform. The boom, con-
trolled either from the base or the platform, can be
raised to 85 ft.

FIRE FIGHTING

A number of vehicles have been specially developed for fighting fires. A major task of these is to throw a jet of water a long distance and thus they require powerful pumps. In order to be able to rescue people trapped in upper floors, or to provide a platform from which water can be directed down into the heart of a fire, long ladders are also an essential piece of equipment.

Other equipment includes nets and jump sheets, to catch people escaping from upper floors, first aid kits and smoke masks for the firemen. Some fire engines, for example those designed to fight forest fires, or burning aircraft, carry their own supply of water, but most city fire engines use the water-mains.

TRADITIONAL PUMP/ESCAPE TENDER

FIRE CRASH TENDER. Many aircraft fire engines carry their own liquid and have powerful gun-like monitors to spray a jet of foam. The Thorneycroft Nubian crash tender holds 5,000 gallons and has a range of 100 ft.

NORTH SEA RIG. This rig is of the fixed type, supported by legs resting on the sea bed. Operations in the North Sea are particularly hazardous, with winds gusting up to 100 m.p.h. and waves 40 ft. high.
In the search for supplies of natural gas, some rigs have capsized and several members of their crews have lost their lives.

DRILLING RIGS

In the search for oil and gas, special rigs have been developed to permit drilling off coast-lines under the sea. These consist basically of a large platform supported by three or more huge legs or cassions. The platform supports the drilling rig and contains the living quarters for the crew.

While drilling is in progress, the rigs can either float at anchor, like a big ship, or the legs can be lowered on to the sea bed.

Most drilling rigs have a helicopter landing pad to facilitate the supply of provisions and relief crews. They are also useful if the rig has to be evacuated quickly in an emergency.

A major problem with drilling rigs is that they have to be towed to the desired drilling sites, and they do not make good ships. When under tow there is always the danger of a sudden storm which could cause the rig to capsize.

A North Sea gas drilling rig under tow. Costing millions of pounds, this type of rig has a crew of 60 men and can drill to depths of up to 20,000 ft, or nearly four miles. The rig measures over 300 ft from corner to corner and weighs 15,000 tons.

LEFT: DRILL: Holman Holtrac.
Drill diameter: 4 in. Hole depth: 60-80 in.
A 37 h.p. compressor supplies power for the drill.

CENTRE: DUMPER TRUCK: Aveling-Barford.
Engine: 476 h.p.   Speed: 33 m.p.h.
Capacity: 35 tons.

RIGHT: ELECTRIC SHOVEL: Ruston-Bucyrus 110-RB.
Engine: 528 h.p.   Bucket capacity: 6-7 tons.

QUARRYING

As with coal mining, many big machines are used for quarrying. Two basic machines are required. One to dig or pick up the ore, and one to carry the ore away. Power shovels are usually used for the former task. In the early days these were steam powered, but these have now been replaced by diesel-electric machines. Explosives are often used to break up the ore into manageable chunks and special machines are used to drill the deep holes in which the explosives are placed for blasting.

For the rapid removal of the overburden, that is, of the layer of soil covering a seam of coal or ore, machines known as bucket wheel excavators are often used. A typical bucket wheel machine, made by the German firm of Krupp, is shown below. This has eight buckets, each of $\frac{1}{2}$ ton capacity. The soil is conveyed from the wheel by a conveyor belt and dumped over a mile away.

OPEN CAST MINING. The biggest machines are the giant drag-lines used in open cast mining, that is, the mining of coal, iron, clay and other minerals near the surface. These huge machines consist of a long jib pivoting on a massive mobile base. A bucket is lowered to the ground and then pulled or dragged along the ground until it is full. When full, the load is hauled up and swung round for dumping, either on the ground, or if required, into trucks so that it can be carried away.

Shown below is the Ransome Rapier W1800 Walking Drag-line. At one time this was the biggest machine of its type working in Britain. It weighs 1800 tons, has a boom length of 245 ft. and a bucket capacity of 60 tons.

An automatic coal cutting machine is illustrated on the opposite page. The coal is cut and loaded automatically. When the cutter has been backwards and forwards once, the whole machine, complete with roof supports, advances into the seam ready for another cut. Below is the remote control panel.

3
Artefacts

lthough somewhat weathered by age, there are a number of surviving artefacts of Celtic origin. Some of these were buried with their owners; many, especially in Britain, have been recovered from lakes and rivers where they had been thrown during some ritual. Some stonework still survives, often in the form of crosses.

Decoration on the artefacts includes spirals, curves, leaves, scrolls, trumpets, palmettes (ornamental shapes like palms), triskeles (patterns with three legs radiating from a centre), and many zoomorphic creatures. The designs are often symmetrical.

Many of the artefacts taken from men's graves are items of war. Iron, bronze, gold and silver swords, helmets, daggers and adornments from horses and chariots were often elaborately decorated with wonderful patterns. Many of the designs in this book have been inspired by these.

In women's graves, jewellery, torques (twisted metal necklaces or collars) and other accessories, such as bronze mirrors, have been discovered. Some later objects, especially brooches and pins, were enamelled in red, blue and yellow. Although these pins usually had a practical purpose, such as holding items of clothing together, they were also works of art in themselves. Cauldrons and coins were decorated too.

There are still many stone crosses to be found throughout the British Isles, especially in Ireland. Earlier stone crosses were just slabs of stone, carved with simple spirals and knots, but later the stone itself was carved into the shape of a cross, then elaborately decorated, not only with patterns but with significant religious pictures. The site of these crosses often became the place where people met for prayer. There are still some carved stone heads remaining.

Wool Pincushion and Scissors-keeper

These are worked in tent stitch on 14# canvas. They are simple designs, but are made more interesting partly by the colouring and partly by the use of soft cotton to contrast with the wool. When the pincushion design was complete, I stitched a piece of cord around the edges, then made tassels from the left-over wool and fastened one at each corner. Alternatively, beads could be used instead of tassels.

The scissors-keeper is really a tiny cushion which you attach to your scissors with a 45cm (17¹¹⁄₁₆in) length of cord or twisted cord. This prevents these valuable tools from slipping down the side of the chair-cushion. It also acts as a temporary place to stick your needle when the phone rings. I worked a plain cream back for my cushion, but a heavy cotton fabric would be a good substitute.

Wool Pincushion

Design size
10 x 10cm
(3⅞ x 3⅞in)

Stitch count
55 x 55

Materials
14# canvas

Thread required

	Anchor Tapisserie Wool	Anchor Soft Cotton	Strands for tent stitch	Amount
		386	1	362.1cm (142½in)
	9800		1	151.2cm (59½in)
	8424		1	31.5cm (12⅞in)
	8422		1	32.9cm (12¹⁵⁄₁₆in)
	8506		1	29.2cm (11½in)
	8610		1	31.5cm (12⅜in)
	8608		1	32.9cm (12¹⁵⁄₁₆in)
	8606		1	29.2cm (11½in)

(1 skein of each of these threads will stitch both designs)

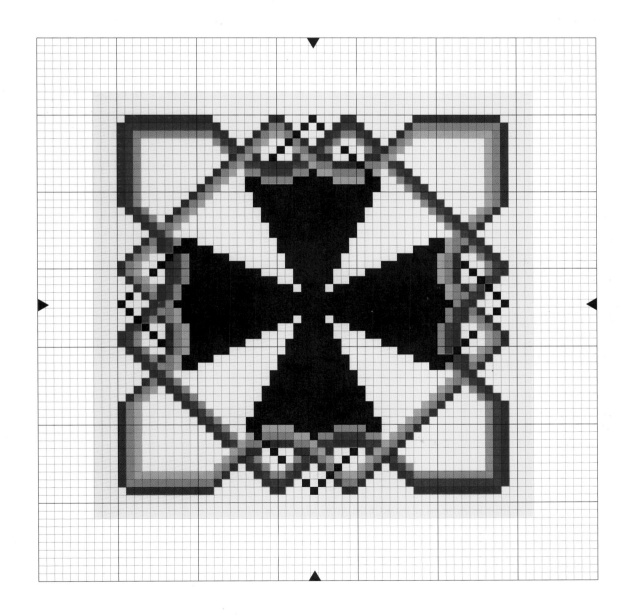

Scissors-keeper

Design size
4.4 x 4.4cm
(1¾ x 1¾in)

Stitch count
24 x 24

Materials
14# canvas

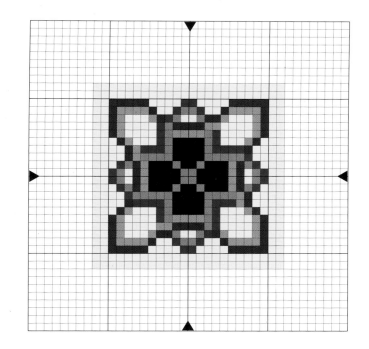

Thread required

	Anchor Tapisserie Wool	Anchor Soft Cotton	Strands for tent stitch	Amount
		386	1	66.7cm (26¼in)
	9800		1	13cm (5⅛in)
	8424		1	10.2cm (4in)
	8506		1	13cm (5⅛in)
	8610		1	16.7cm (6⁹⁄₁₆in)
	8606		1	13.9cm (5⁷⁄₁₆in)

Other ideas for the designs
• coasters worked in stranded cotton
  on Aida
• card and gift tag
• potpourri cushion

Two Finger Plates

The design for the first finger plate came from a 4th century French torque, and a German bronze scabbard plate was the inspiration for the second. They are worked on 14# 55mm (2⅛in) Aida band as this fits exactly into the finger plates and already has an edging. When the stitching was complete, I ironed a strip of Vilene on to the back to make the bands firmer and stop them from fraying.

1

Design size
5.1 x 24.3cm
(2 x 9%₁₆in)

Stitch count
28 x 134

Materials
14# 55mm (2⅛in)
Aida band

2

Design size
4.9 x 24.5cm
(1⅞ x 9⅝in)

Stitch count
27 x 135

Materials
14# 55mm (2⅛in)
Aida band

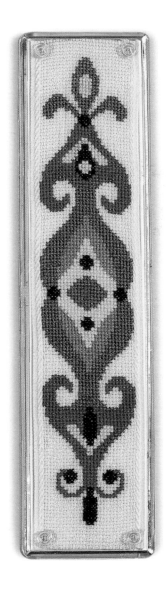

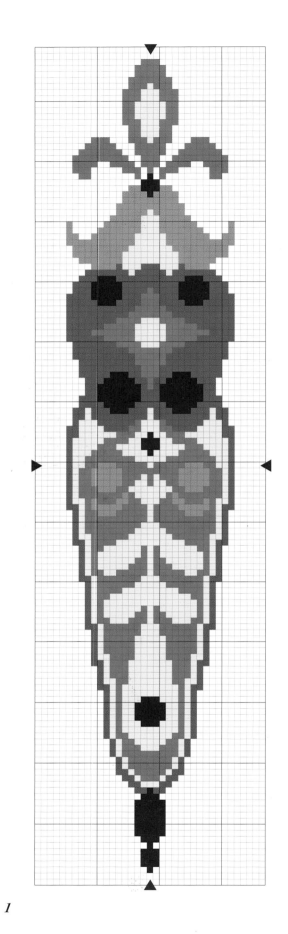

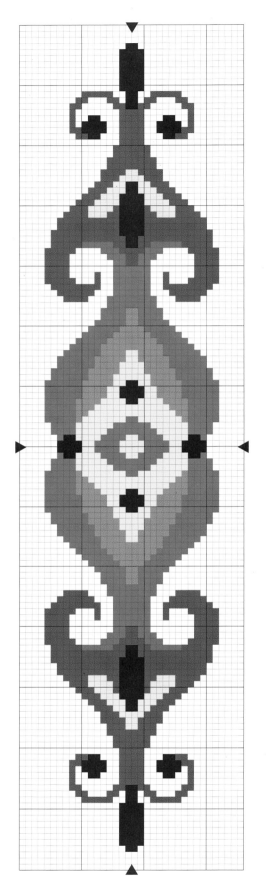

1

2

1
Thread required

	Anchor Tapisserie Wool	Strands for cross stitch	Amount
	403	2	111.1cm (43¾in)
	896	2	324.1cm (127$\frac{9}{16}$in)
	895	2	114.8cm (45$\frac{3}{16}$in)
	779	2	300.1cm (118⅛in)
	386	2	150cm (59in)

(1 skein of each of these threads is enough to stitch both designs)

2
Thread required

	Anchor Tapisserie Wool	Strands for cross stitch	Amount
	403	2	93.1cm (36⅝in)
	896	2	253.3cm (99$\frac{11}{16}$in)
	895	2	112.5cm (44$\frac{5}{16}$in)
	779	2	343.1cm (135$\frac{1}{16}$in)
	386	2	288.9cm (113¾in)

Other ideas for these designs
- bookmarks
- mini bell pulls

Cosmetic Bag and Beaded Card

Both of these designs are derived from bronze-covered iron helmets from France. The beads give added interest to the designs. The cosmetic bag was worked on a denim-blue ready-made bag from Fabric Flair and the design in the cream card (from Impress) was worked on 16# Aida. Use a single strand of matching cotton to stitch the beads on.

Cosmetic Bag

Design size
6.9 x 9.4cm
(2¹¹⁄₁₆ x 3¹¹⁄₁₆in)

Stitch count
38 x 52

Materials
14# fabric
114 Mill Hill
Beads No. 03034

Beaded Card

Design size
6.4 x 7.6cm
(2½ x 3in)

Stitch count
40 x 48

Materials
16# Aida
287 Mill Hill
Beads No. 03035

Cosmetic Bag
Thread required

Anchor Stranded Cotton	Strands for cross stitch	Amount
1	2	275.1cm (108⅝in)

Cosmetic Bag

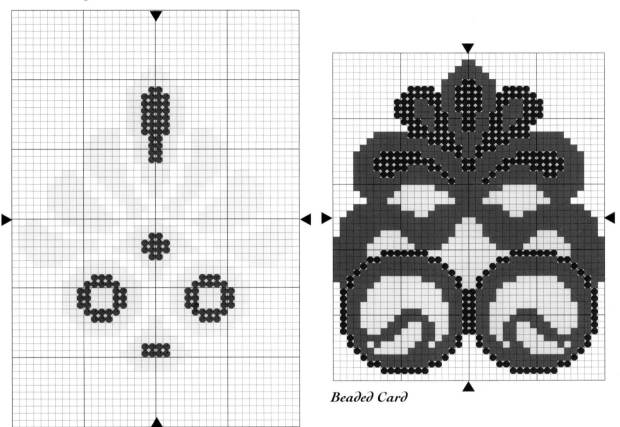

Beaded Card

Beaded card
Thread required

Anchor Stranded Cotton	Strands for cross stitch	Amount
386	2	142.6cm (56⅛in)
1074	2	328.2cm (129³⁄₁₆in)

Other ideas for these designs
- cards
- pincushion or potpourri cushion
- lid for a pot

mini Bell pull

This is worked over 2 threads on 28# coffee-coloured Jobelan which shows off the colours. It was designed using several decorated letters from the *Book of Kells* and the *Lindisfarne Gospels* and some from stone carvings. The tiny brass hanger gives the final touch.

Design size
17.8 x 29.2cm
(7 x 11½in)

Stitch count
98 x 161

Materials
28# Jobelan,
coffee

Thread required

	Anchor Stranded cotton	Kreinik	Strands for cross stitch	Amount
	403		2	290.3cm (114⁵⁄₁₆in)
	1		2	344.5cm (135⅝in)
	214		2	147.3cm (58in)
	897		2	34.3cm (13½in)
	217		2	109.3cm (43in)
	123		2	84.7cm (33⁵⁄₁₆in)
	122		2	89.8cm (35⁵⁄₁₆in)
	400		2	75cm (29½in)
	121		2	45.4cm (17⅞in)
		Japan#5	2	29.6cm (11⅝in)

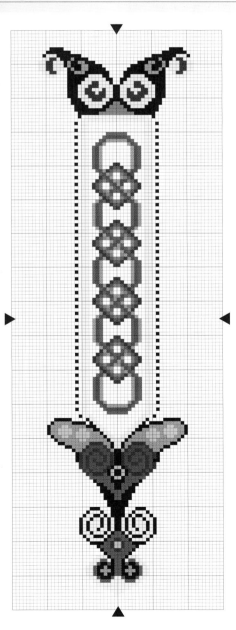

wardrobe hanger

This consists of two scented cushions joined together with ribbon and fastened to a padded coat hanger. It is then hung up in the wardrobe to keep it fresh. Alternatively, if you think it's too nice to be hidden away, hang it in the bedroom or bathroom from a brass ring. Instructions for making up a wardrobe hanger can be found in the Projects section on page 166. The designs for these came from some horse trappings from the Polden Hills in Somerset.

1

Design size
9.6 x 8.9cm
(3¾ x 3½in)

Stitch count
53 x 49

Materials
14# Aida or 28#
Jobelan worked
over 2 threads

2

Design size
8.9 x 8.9cm
(3½ x 3½in)

Stitch count
49 x 49

Materials
14# Aida or 28#
Jobelan worked
over 2 threads

1
Thread required

	Anchor Stranded Cotton	Strands for cross stitch	Amount
	380	2	29.6cm (11⅝in)
	215	2	35.2cm (13¹³⁄₁₆in)
	398	2	43.5cm (17⅛in)
	339	2	486.7cm (191⅝in)
	386	2	207.4cm (81⅝in)

(1 skein of each of these threads will be enough for both designs)

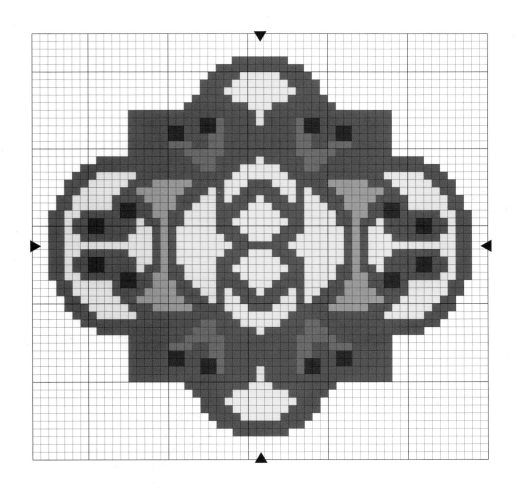

2
Thread required

	Anchor Stranded Cotton	Strands for cross stitch	Amount
	380	2	22.2cm (8¾in)
	215	2	68.5cm (26¹⁵⁄₁₆in)
	398	2	122.2cm (48⅛in)
	400	2	65.8cm (25⅞in)
	339	2	387.6cm (152⁹⁄₁₆in)
	386	2	121.3cm (47¾in)

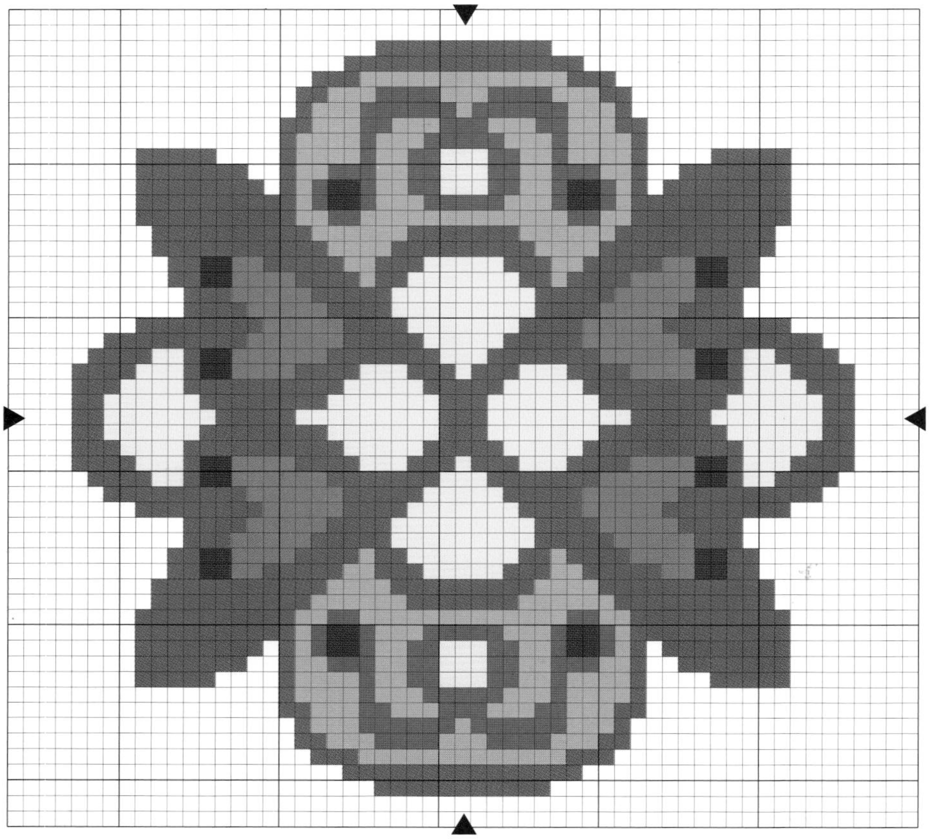

Other ideas for these designs
- cards
- lids for pots
- small pictures
- teapot stands

Beaded Lid for an elm pot

This design, inspired by a stone cross, is stitched on 18# Aida in a stunning mixture of purple and cream with beads in the centre. I have made it up into the lid for a lovely elm pot, which has an aperture of 9cm (3⁹⁄₁₆in) diameter.

Design size
7.6 x 7.6cm
(3 x 3in)

Stitch count
54 x 54

Materials
18# Aida
32 Mill Hill Beads
No. 03034

Thread required

	Anchor Stranded Cotton	Strands for cross stitch	Amount
■	102	2	131.5cm (51¾in)
■	99	2	119.6cm (47⅟₁₆in)
■	97	2	102.6cm (40⅜in)
	386	2	291cm (114⁹⁄₁₆in)

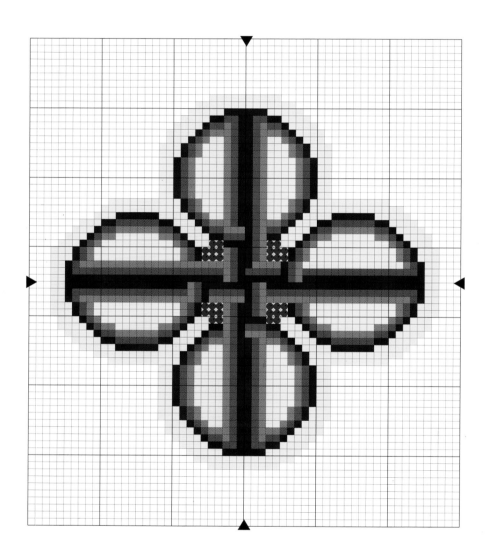

Other ideas for this design
- card
- cosmetic bag
- pincushion

Bookmark in Pinks

This design came from a French torque. It is shown here worked onto a white, ready-made bookmark. I ironed a piece of Vilene on the back to make it firmer.

Design size
4.1 x 14.3cm
(1⅝ x 5⅝in)

Stitch count
29 x 101

Materials
18# fabric

Thread required

	Anchor Stranded Cotton	Strands for cross stitch	Amount
■	70	2	101.9cm (40⅛in)
■	66	2	119.6cm (47¹⁄₁₆in)
■	386	2	40.3cm (15⅞in)
■	69	2	203.1cm (79¹⁵⁄₁₆in)

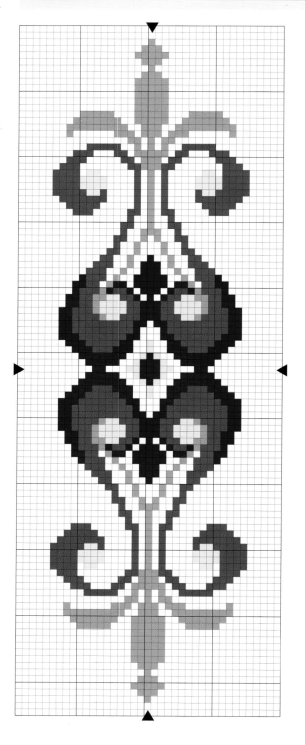

Other ideas for this design
• turned horizontally it becomes a border
• door plate
• small bell pull; add some beads
• picture

5th Century Strip Picture

T his adaptation from a 5th century German metal strip is stitched on 19# Easistitch from Fabric Flair. It has a rich combination of colours and could easily be enhanced with some gold and beads.

Design size
5.5 x 17.5cm
(2⅛ x 6⅞in)

Stitch count
41 x 131

Materials
19# Easistitch

Thread required

	Anchor Stranded Cotton	Strands for cross stitch	Amount
■	403	2	195.8cm (77¹⁄₁₆in)
	386	2	27.3cm (10¾in)
■	215	2	85.6cm (33¹¹⁄₁₆in)
■	217	2	171.6cm (67⁹⁄₁₆in)
■	99	2	42.7cm (16¹³⁄₁₆in)
■	87	2	46.1cm (18⅛in)
■	102	2	265.5cm (104½in)

Other ideas for this design
- small bell pull
- finger plate

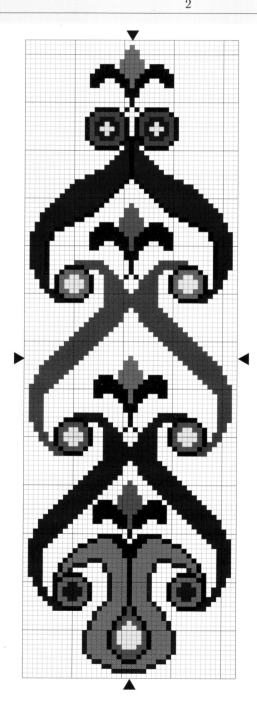

Two Christmas
Potpourri Cushions

I took the designs for these from some Scottish stone crosses and was originally going to make ordinary potpourri cushions, but when I saw them stitched I couldn't resist turning them into scented Christmas hangers. They would make lovely stocking-fillers, or could be hung upon the tree. I used a printed Christmas fabric to finish them off. They were stitched on 28# Jobelan worked over 2 threads.

1

Design size
8.3 x 8.3cm
(3¼ x 3¼in)

Stitch count
46 x 46

Materials
28# Jobelan

2

Design size
9.1 x 9.1cm
(3⁹⁄₁₆ x 3⁹⁄₁₆in)

Stitch count
50 x 50

Materials
28# Jobelan,
worked over 2
threads

1
Thread required

	Anchor Stranded Cotton	Kreinik	Strands for cross stitch	Amount
	47		2	167.2cm (65¹³⁄₁₆in)
	227		2	129.7cm (51¹⁄₁₆in)
		Japan#5	2	147.7cm (58⅛in)

(1 skein of each of these threads will be enough to stitch both designs)

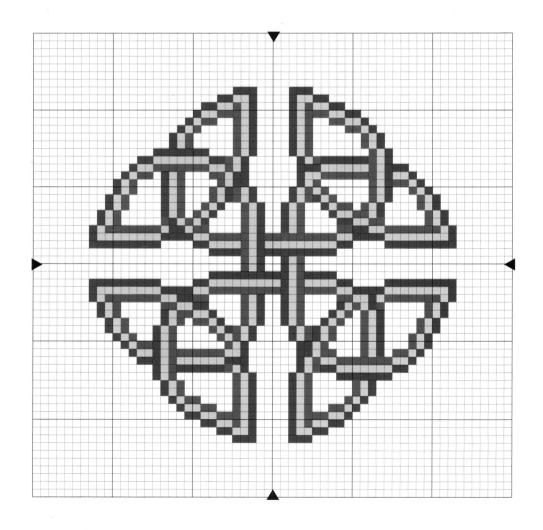

2
Thread required

	Anchor Stranded Cotton	Kreinik	Strands for cross stitch	Amount
	47		2	245.4cm (96⅝in)
	227		2	188cm (74in)
		Japan#5	2	245.4cm (96⅝in)

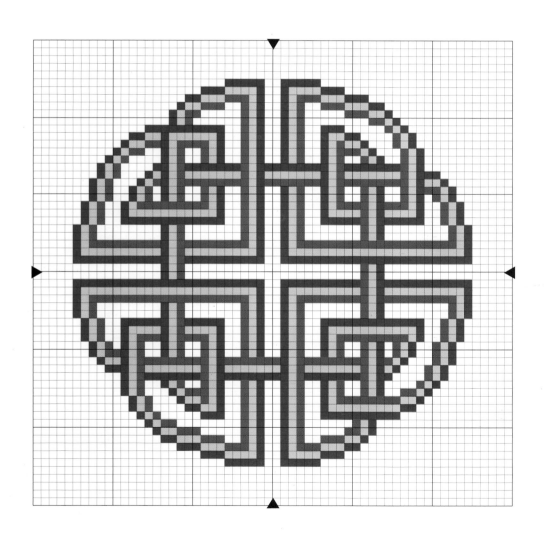

Two Notebook holders

S till on the theme of Christmas, here are two useful, but small, gifts that will not take long to stitch. They were both stitched on 19# Easistitch and are very quick to make up into notebooks. The green design came from a sword handle and the salmon one from a 5th century Bohemian brooch.

Green design

Design size
3.1 x 7cm
(1³⁄₁₆ x 2¾in)

Stitch count
23 x 52

Materials
19# Easistitch

Salmon design

Design size
3.7 x 6.7cm
(1⁷⁄₁₆ x 2⅝in)

Stitch count
28 x 50

Materials
19# Easistitch

Green Design
Thread required

	Anchor Stranded Cotton	Strands for cross stitch	Amount
	244	2	18.4cm (7¼in)
	878	2	122.8cm (48⅜in)
	297	2	8.2cm (3³⁄₁₆in)

Salmon Design
Thread required

	Anchor Stranded Cotton	Strands for cross stitch	Amount
	403	2	84.6cm (33⅜in)
	11	2	154.2cm (60¹¹⁄₁₆in)
	8	2	42.3cm (16⅝in)

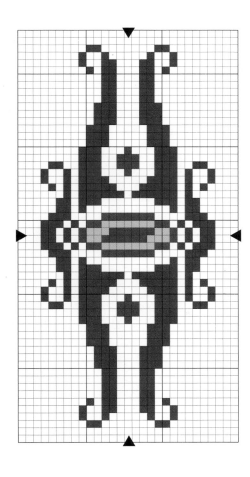

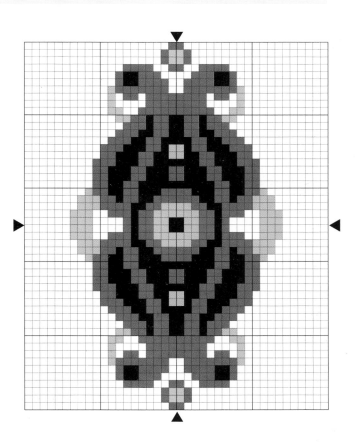

Other ideas for these small designs
- fridge magnets
- cards
- spectacles case
- key ring

Lid for a Crystal Pot

The design for the lid of this beautiful crystal pot came from the pattern on a Bavarian pottery bowl. It has a touch of metallic thread, which gives it a sparkle, and if this were changed to silver or gold the pot would make a very personal anniversary gift. It was worked on 22# Aida.

Design size
5.5 x 5.5cm
(2⅛ x 2⅛in)

Stitch count
48 x 48

Materials
22# Aida

Thread required

	Anchor Stranded Cotton	Kreinik	Strands for cross stitch	Amount
	127		2	103.7cm (40¹³⁄₁₆in)
	386		2	33cm (13in)
	158		2	121.4cm (47¹³⁄₁₆in)
	168		2	93.1cm (36⅝in)
		Blending Filament 014	2	9.4cm (3¹¹⁄₁₆in)

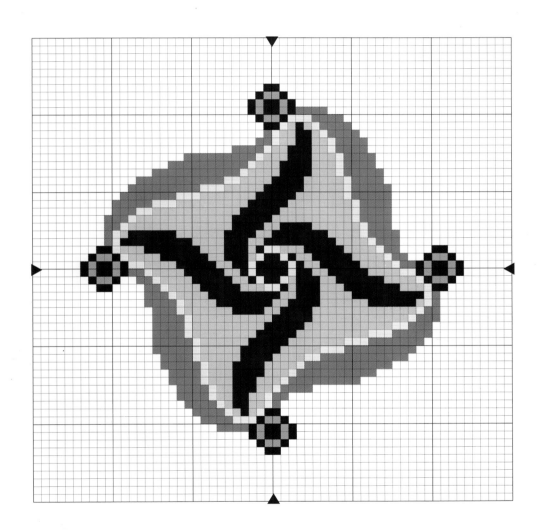

Other ideas for this design
- anniversary card
- potpourri sachet

Tote Bag Pocket

I used this design in conjunction with two borders to make a tote bag large enough to take my tapestry on its frame. See page 108 for the border design. I added a pocket inside for the threads and two smaller pockets on the outside to store my scissors, spare needles and those numerous smaller items! The pocket is worked on 28# Jobelan over two threads in colours to match the borders. I just had to include this design as it came from a scabbard found at Wetwang in the East Riding of Yorkshire, which is close to where I live.

Design size
7.3 x 10cm (2⅞ x 3¹⁵⁄₁₆in)

Stitch count
40 x 55

Materials
28# Jobelan

Thread required

	Anchor Stranded Cotton	Strands for cross stitch	Amount
	403	2	63.4cm (24¹⁵⁄₁₆in)
	189	2	122.2cm (48⅛in)
	186	2	105.6cm (41⁶⁄₁₆in)
	69	2	69.5cm (27⅜in)
	66	2	76.9cm (30¼in)

(1 skein of each of these threads will be enough to stitch the tote bag pocket and the potpourri sac which follows)

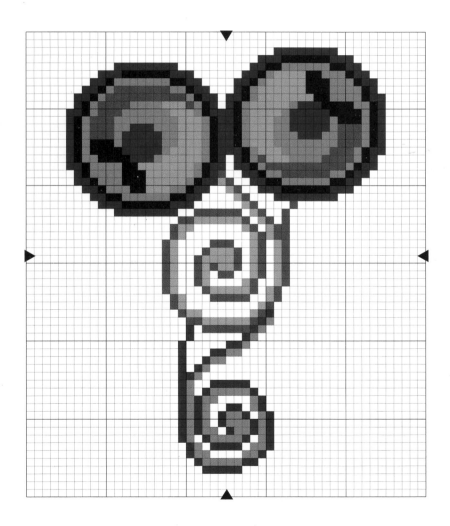

Small Potpourri Sac

This is a very useful small design that I have stitched in colours to match the previous item. I keep it in my stitching bag to scent my work and keep the moths away. It would also be useful in a drawer.

Design size
3.4 x 4cm
(1⁵⁄₁₆ x 1⁹⁄₁₆in)

Stitch count
19 x 22

Materials
14# fabric

Thread required

	Anchor Stranded Cotton	Strands for cross stitch	Amount
	403	2	31.5cm (12⅜in)
	189	2	30.1cm (11¹³⁄₁₆in)
	186	2	12cm (4¹¹⁄₁₆in)
	69	2	16.7cm (6⅝in)
	66	2	12cm (4¹¹⁄₁₆in)

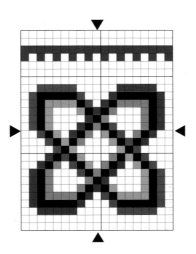

Other ideas for the design

- fridge magnet
- key ring
- paperweight
- gift tag

palmette Card

This was based on a German palmette design. Stitched on 16# Aida, it makes a dramatic and original card.

Design size
7.5 x 7.9cm
(2¹⁵⁄₁₆ x 3⅛in)

Stitch count
47 x 50

Materials
16# Aida

Thread required

	Anchor Stranded Cotton	Strands for cross stitch	Amount
■	403	2	144.2cm (56¾in)
□	1	2	77.8cm (30⅝in)
■	217	2	81cm (31⅞in)
■	897	2	109.4cm (43⅛in)
■	121	2	51.5cm (20¼in)
■	123	2	109.4cm (43⅛in)

Beaded
Herb Cushion

T his design came from a helmet design. Stitched on 14# in these salmon
colours, it makes a pretty sachet to hang in a wardrobe or other cupboard,
and it can either be stuffed with dried herbs or with a filling scented with
herbal oil. You could put a tassel at the bottom or matching beads.

Design size
9.1 x 9.1cm
(3⁹⁄₁₆ x 3⁹⁄₁₆in)

Stitch count
50 x 50

Materials
.14# Aida, or 28#
Jobelan stitched
over 2 threads
116 Mill Hill
Beads No 03057

Thread required

Anchor Stranded Cotton	Strands for cross stitch	Amount
236	2	131.5cm (51¾in)
8	2	75.9cm (29⅞in)
386	2	345.4cm (136in)
10	2	145.4cm (57¼in)
13	2	143.5cm (56½in)

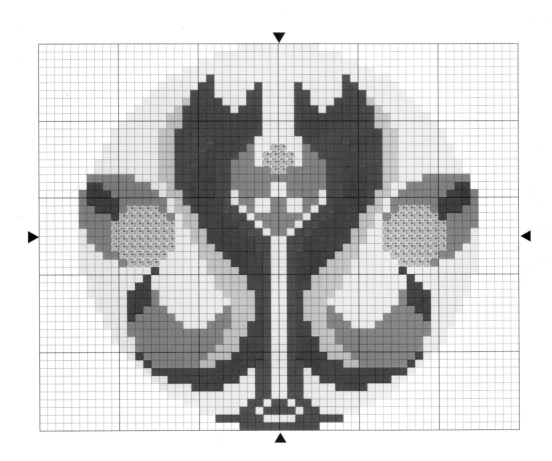

Damask Cushion with Matching Lavender Sac

This cushion is stitched on a damask square which already has a defined stitching area. Made up using ribbons and lace, it creates a delicate cushion for a bedroom. The lavender sac is made from 28# Jobelan worked over two threads. This design matches the duvet and pillow bands on page 111.

Design size
2.7 x 3.5cm
(1¹⁄₁₆ x 1⅜in)

Stitch count
17 x 22

Materials
Damask Cushion:
Circle of damask embroidery fabric
Lavender Sac: 28# Jobelan, worked over 2 threads

Thread required

	Anchor Stranded Cotton	Strands for cross stitch	Amount
▨	896	2	5.3cm (2⅟₁₆in)
▨	895	2	9.7cm (3¹³⁄₁₆in)
▨	216	2	38.9cm (15⅝in)
▨	386	2	5.3cm (2⅟₁₆in)

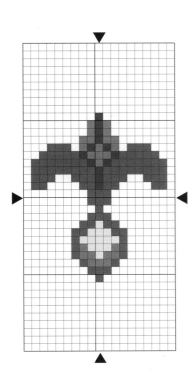

Other ideas for this small design
- place setting
- gift tag
- pendant
- key ring

Fluted
Paperweight

This design was worked on 22#
Aida to fit the fluted glass
paperweight. It is striking
worked in these purples and is
easy to make up.

Design size
5.8 x 5.8cm
(2¼ x 2¼in)

Stitch count
50 x 50

Materials
22# Aida

Thread required

	Anchor Stranded Cotton	Strands for cross stitch	Amount
■	403	2	146.2cm (57⁹⁄₁₆in)
□	1	2	62.5cm (24⅝in)
■	119	2	122.6cm (48¼in)
■	118	2	155.6cm (61¼in)
■	117	2	83.7cm (32¹⁵⁄₁₆in)

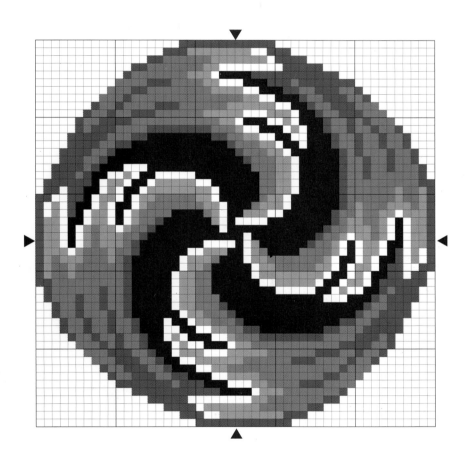

Other ideas for this design
- round card
- lid for a pot

Lid for a Black Pot

Chis stylish design was worked on 16# Hardanger. The glossy black pot with its cream lid would add a touch of luxury to any room. The black pot has an aperture which is 9cm (3⁹⁄₁₆in) in diameter.

Design size
7.9 x 7.9cm
(3⅛ x 3⅛in)

Stitch count
50 x 50

Materials
16# Hardanger

Thread required

	Anchor Stranded Cotton	Strands for cross stitch	Amount
■	403	2	1.6cm (⅝in)
■	217	2	51.1cm (20⅛in)
■	215	2	46.2cm (18⅜in)
■	340	2	119.9cm (47³⁄₁₆in)
■	338	2	111.8cm (44in)
■	337	2	102.9cm (40½in)
■	123	2	51.1cm (20⅛in)
■	121	2	46.2cm (18⅜in)
■	386	2	230.9cm (90⅞in)

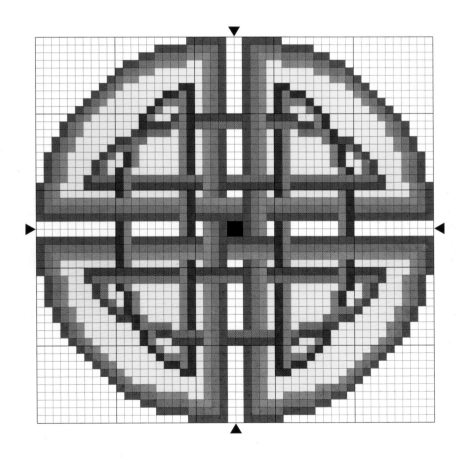

4
Triangular Knots

There are countless examples of plaits and knots in the Celtic heritage. Some of these are basic and unadorned, like those engraved in stonework, but others, as in the illuminated manuscripts, are more developed and highly decorated. Many of them would need to be reproduced in stitching on an impracticably large scale to do them justice.

Although there are more complicated patterns in the book, I decided that the triquetra (three interlaced arcs) knot was basically a simple enough shape to be developed into a large bold item worked in wool on canvas. Variations on the original knot, with the addition of a simple border, have made a lovely wool rug, which could easily be adapted to fit into any colour scheme. Details of the rug are to be found in the projects section of the book.

The simplicity of these designs has made them easy to work and quick to stitch with multi-coloured threads, to develop into cushions, pictures and cards.

ҚHOTS 1–6

αny of these knot designs can be made into burgundy or jade cushion centres or pictures just by changing the thread and the fabric. As rugknots they are worked on 10# using 1 strand. The cushion centres are worked in cross stitch over two threads on 14# Jobelan using two strands. The pictures are in half cross stitch worked on 22# canvas using three strands. The charts for these knots can be found on pages 158–9. Details of how to stitch the rug are on page 157.

Knots as Pictures

Design size
12.1 x 10.5cm
(4¾ x 4⅛in)

Stitch count
105 x 91

Materials
Mono canvas 22#

Thread required for each design
Jade

	Anchor Stranded Cotton	Strands for cross stitch	Amount
	683	3	222.8cm (87¹¹⁄₁₆in)
	879	3	213.5 cm (84⅛in)
	877	3	205.5cm (80⅞in)
	876	3	197.6cm (77¹³⁄₁₆in)
	875	3	191.4cm (75⅜in)

Burgundy

	Anchor Stranded Cotton	Strands for cross stitch	Amount
	72	3	222.8cm (87¹¹⁄₁₆in)
	1019	3	213.5 cm (84⅛in)
	1018	3	205.5cm (80⅞in)
	1017	3	197.6cm (77¹³⁄₁₆in)
	1016	3	191.4cm (75⅜in)

Knots as Cushions

Design size
19 x 16.5cm
(7½ x 6½in)

Stitch count
105 x 91

Materials
Jobelan 28#,
worked over two
threads

Thread required for each design
Jade

	Anchor Stranded Cotton	Strands for cross stitch	Amount
	683	2	233.4cm (91⅞in)
	879	2	223.7cm (88¹⁄₁₆in)
	877	2	215.3cm (84¾in)
	876	2	207cm (81½in)
	875	2	200.5cm (78¹⁵⁄₁₆in)

Burgundy

	Anchor Stranded Cotton	Strands for cross stitch	Amount
	72	2	233.4cm (91⅞in)
	1019	2	223.7cm (88¹⁄₁₆in)
	1018	2	215.3cm (84¾in)
	1017	2	207cm (81½in)
	1016	2	200.5cm (78¹⁵⁄₁₆in)

Knots as Rugknots

The instructions for making the rug are on page 157.

Thread required

Colour	Anchor Tapisserie Wool (jade)	Anchor Tapisserie Wool (burgundy)
Very dark	8884	8514
Dark	8882	8512
Medium	8880	8510
Light	8878	8506
Pale	8874	8502

The amount of thread needed for each square is given on page 157.

velvet knot Cushions

αs soon as I saw the wonderful colour variations in Bond Multi's Embellishment Yarn, I imagined it being used for these designs, and the completed cushions were not disappointing. With the rich, deep greeny blue velvet backing, they really look luxurious and worthy of a place in any home. They were worked on 14# Aida.

knots 7-12

Knot 7
Thread required

	Anchor Stranded Cotton	Bond Multi	Strands for cross stitch	Amount
▬	403*		1	176.6cm (69½in)
▬		Embellishment Yarn Gemstone 1096	1	253.8cm (99¹⁵⁄₁₆in)

*2 Strands for back stitch (1 skein of 403 is enough to complete knots 7–12)

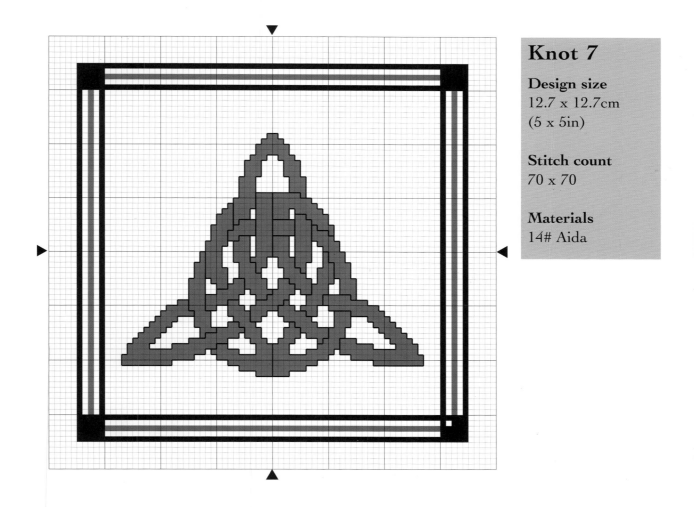

Knot 7

Design size
12.7 x 12.7cm
(5 x 5in)

Stitch count
70 x 70

Materials
14# Aida

Knot 8

Design size
9.1 x 8cm
(3⁹⁄₁₆ x 3⅛in)

Stitch count
50 x 44

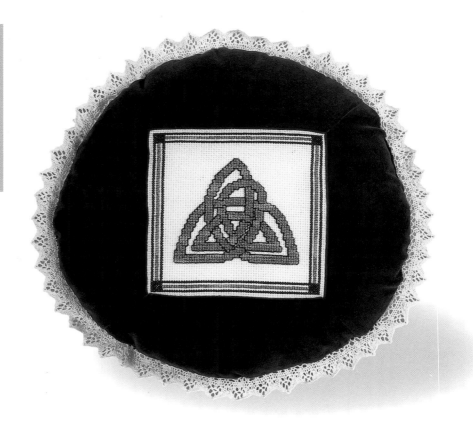

Knot 9

Design size
8.7 x 8.3cm
(3⅜ x 3¼in)

Stitch count
48 x 46

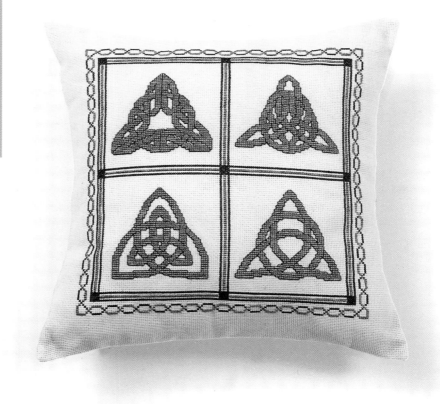

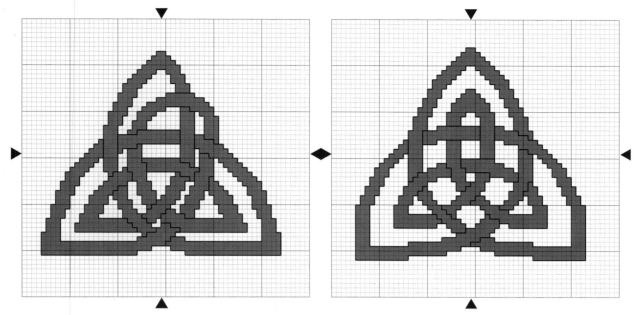

Knot 8   *Knot 9*

Knot 8
Thread required

	Anchor Stranded Cotton	Bond Multi	Strands for cross stitch	Amount
■	403*			44.1cm (17⅜in)
■		1096	1	214.6cm (84½in)

*2 Strands for back stitch

Knot 9
Thread required

	Anchor Stranded Cotton	Bond Multi	Strands for cross stitch	Amount
■	403*			44.4cm (17½in)
■		1096	1	201.7cm (79⅜in)

*2 Strands for back stitch

Knot 10

Design size
9.8 x 8.3cm
(3¹³⁄₁₆ x 3¼in)

Stitch count
54 x 46

Knot 11

Design size
9.4 x 8.2cm
(3¹¹⁄₁₆ x 3³⁄₁₆in)

Stitch count
52 x 45

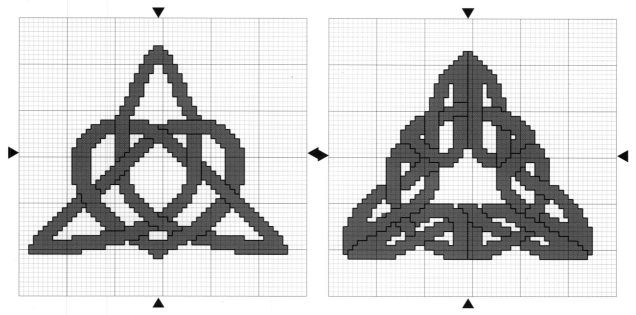

Knot 10

Knot 11

Knot 10
Thread required

	Anchor Stranded Cotton	Bond Multi	Strands for cross stitch	Amount
	403*			39.6cm (15⁹⁄₁₆in)
		1096	1	186.6cm (73⁷⁄₁₆in)

*2 Strands for back stitch

Knot 11
Thread required

	Anchor Stranded Cotton	Bond Multi	Strands for cross stitch	Amount
	403*			46.2cm (18³⁄₁₆in)
		1096	1	247.3cm (97³⁄₈in)

*2 Strands for back stitch

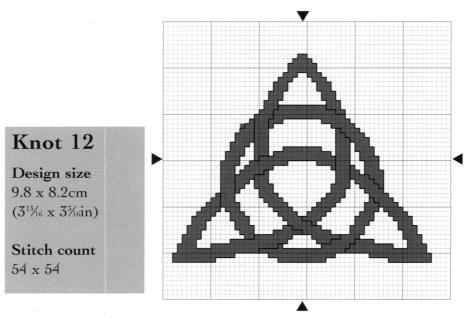

Knot 12

Design size
9.8 x 8.2cm
(3¹³⁄₁₆ x 3³⁄₁₆in)

Stitch count
54 x 54

Knot 12

Knot 12
Thread required

	Anchor Stranded Cotton	Bond Multi	Strands for cross stitch	Amount
	403*			40.2cm (15¹³⁄₁₆in)
		1096	1	183.8cm (72⅜in)

*2 Strands for back stitch

Other ideas for the knot designs

- a bell pull with the designs arranged vertically enclosed by a border
- a set of glass mats. Use a variegated stranded cotton and Aida.

5
Zoomorphic and Anthropomorphic Designs

These are mainly abstract designs incorporating animal and human forms. Many of the designs in this section originate from the *Book of Kells* and the *Lindisfarne Gospels*; their decorated pages are full of patterns interwoven with animal, bird, fish and human figures. Some have symbolic meanings, whereas others appear to be purely ornamental.

Most of these have enough characteristics for the creatures to be identifiable, although they are reproduced in a stylized form. The zoomorphic designs mainly represent lions, hounds, wolves, peacocks, eagles and fish. These are grossly distorted, so that although some part of them, such as the head, may be recognizable, the bodies and limbs form abstract shapes that are often extended to twist into the plaits and knots.

At first glance the animals appear quite comical, but when you take a closer look, some of them are quite ferocious. They are twisted and contorted into knots and often end up being strangled or bitten either by some other creature or even by themselves!

The people seem more like garden gnomes than human beings. Most of the figures have long hair and beards, elongated bodies, and legs and arms which become individual strands of complex woven patterns. The faces are simply shaped and coloured, but seem full of expression, mainly serious, worried or surprised. None appears happy!

I have tried to select a varied range of designs for this section to give you a taste of these fantastic creatures. There are endless possibilities for their use in stitching.

Six Animal Coasters

These designs were all creatures taken from illuminated manuscripts, especially the *Book of Kells*. They are quick to work on 22# Aida, and are dynamic, especially with a touch of gold thread. They are designed to fit deep, square coasters which measure 8.5 x 8.5cm (3⁵⁄₁₆ x 3⁵⁄₁₆in).

Other ideas for these designs
- cards
- paperweights
- decoration on a pocket
- small potpourri sacs

Coaster 1

Design size
5.5 x 6.0cm
(2⅛ x 2⅜in)

Stitch count
48 x 52

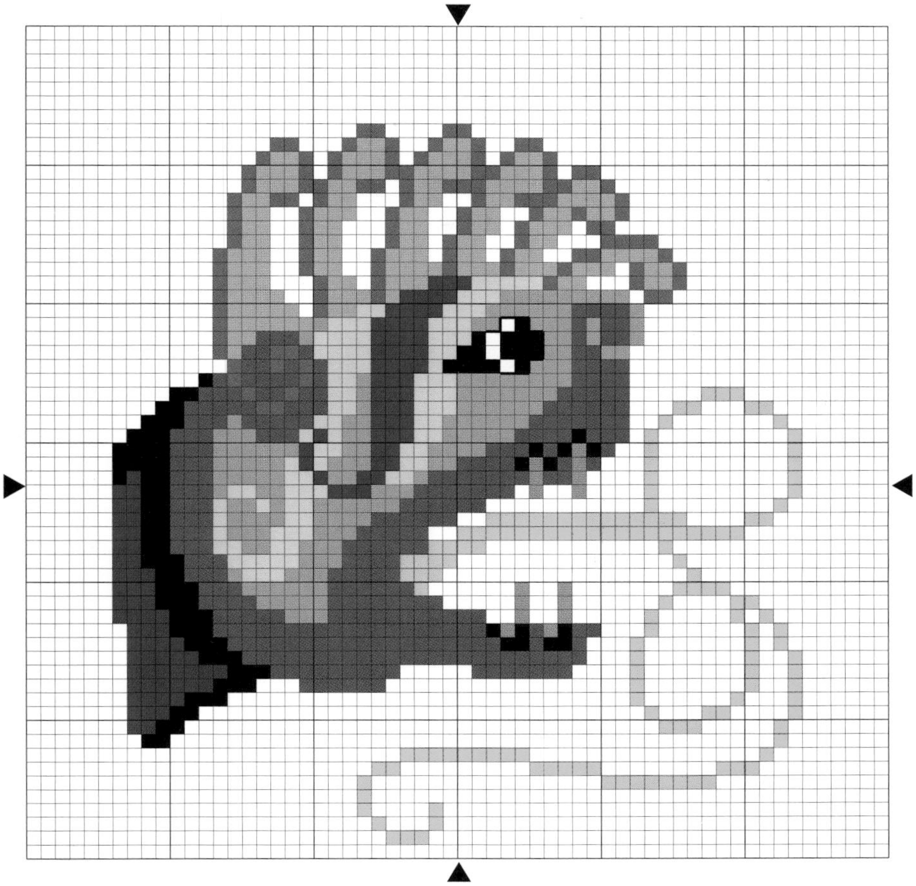

Coaster 1
Thread required

	Anchor Stranded Cotton	Kreinik	Strands for cross stitch	Amount
■	403*		2	29.8cm (11¾in)
□	1		2	1.2cm (7/16in)
■	101		2	89.9cm (35⅜in)
■	890		2	4.4cm (1¾in)
■	298		2	43cm (16 15/16in)
■	1064		2	48.3cm (19in)
■	1068		2	33.9cm (13 5/16in)
■	205		2	34.8cm (13 11/16in)
■	206		2	46.6cm (18 5/16in)
■		Japan#5	2	29.2cm (11½in)

*2 Strands for back stitch (1 skein of each of these threads is enough to complete all six designs)

Coaster 2

Design size
5.7 x 6.1cm
(2¼ x 2⅜in)

Stitch count
49 x 53

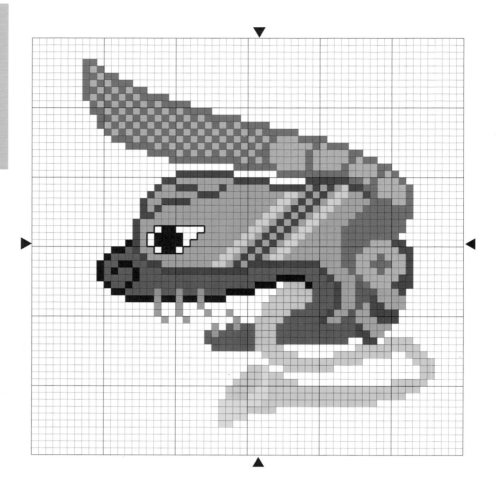

Coaster 2
Thread required

	Anchor Stranded Cotton	Kreinik	Strands for cross stitch	Amount
	403*		2	16.8cm (6⅝in)
	1		2	3.5cm (1⅜in)
	101		2	49.5cm (19½in)
	890		2	5.6cm (2³⁄₁₆in)
	298		2	54.2cm (21⅜in)
	1064		2	79cm (31⅛in)
	1068		2	40.1cm (15¾in)
	205		2	72.8cm (28¹¹⁄₁₆in)
	206		2	50.1cm (19¾in)
		Japan#5	2	19.7cm (7¾in)

*2 Strands for back stitch

Coaster 3

Design size
5.7 x 6.2cm
(2¼ x 2⁷⁄₁₆in)

Stitch count
49 x 54

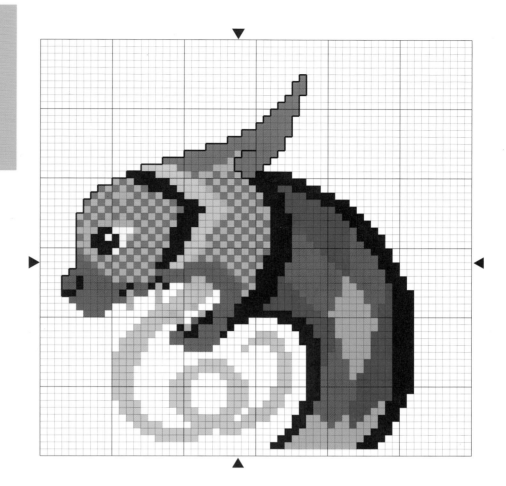

Coaster 3
Thread required

	Anchor Stranded Cotton	Kreinik	Strands for cross stitch	Amount
	403✽		2	98.4cm (38¾in)
	1		2	2.1cm (¹³⁄₁₆in)
	101		2	73.4cm (28⅞in)
	890		2	5.9cm (2⁵⁄₁₆in)
	298		2	59.2cm (23⁵⁄₁₆in)
	1064		2	29.8cm (11¾in)
	1068		2	47.1cm (18⁹⁄₁₆in)
	205		2	60.7cm (23⅞in)
	206		2	39.8cm (15¹¹⁄₁₆in)
		Japan#5	2	13.6cm (5⁵⁄₁₆in)

✽2 Strands for back stitch

Coaster 4

Design size
5.9 x 5.9cm
(2⁵⁄₁₆ x 2⁵⁄₁₆in)

Stitch count
51 x 51

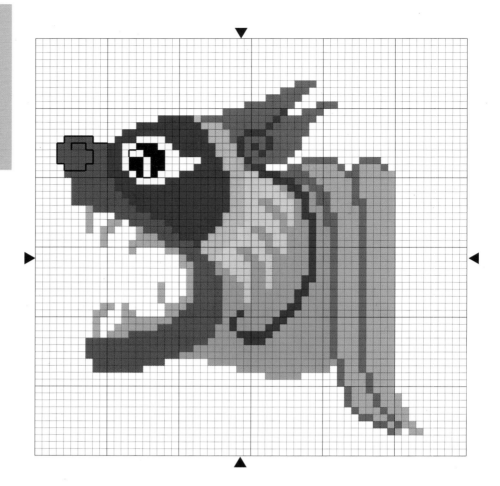

Coaster 4
Thread required

	Anchor Stranded Cotton	Kreinik	Strands for cross stitch	Amount
	403*		2	6.9cm (2¹¹⁄₁₆in)
	1		2	10.3cm (4¹⁄₁₆in)
	101		2	64.5cm (25⅜in)
	890		2	19.2cm (7⁹⁄₁₆in)
	298		2	16.2cm (6⅜in)
	1064		2	82.2cm (32⅜in)
	1068		2	68.7cm (27in)
	205		2	57.7cm (22¹¹⁄₁₆in)
	206		2	77.8cm (30⅝in)
		Japan#5	2	23.9cm (9⅜in)

*2 Strands for back stitch

Coaster 5

Design size
5.9 x 6.2cm
(2⁵⁄₁₆ x 2⁷⁄₁₆in)

Stitch count
51 x 54

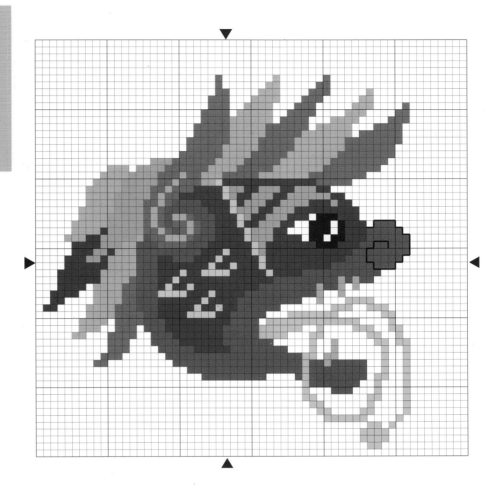

Coaster 5
Thread required

	Anchor Stranded Cotton	Kreinik	Strands for cross stitch	Amount
	403*		2	7.5cm (2¹⁵⁄₁₆in)
	1		2	2.9cm (1⅛in)
	101		2	94.3cm (37⅛in)
	890		2	3.8cm (1½in)
	298		2	34.2cm (13⁷⁄₁₆in)
	1064		2	31.5cm (12⅜in)
	1068		2	97.5cm (38⅜in)
	205		2	78.1cm (30¾in)
	206		2	71cm (27¹⁵⁄₁₆in)
		Japan#5	2	11.2cm (4⅜in)

*2 Strands for back stitch

Coaster 6

Design size
5.7 x 11.1cm
(2¼ x 4⅜in)

Stitch count
49 x 96

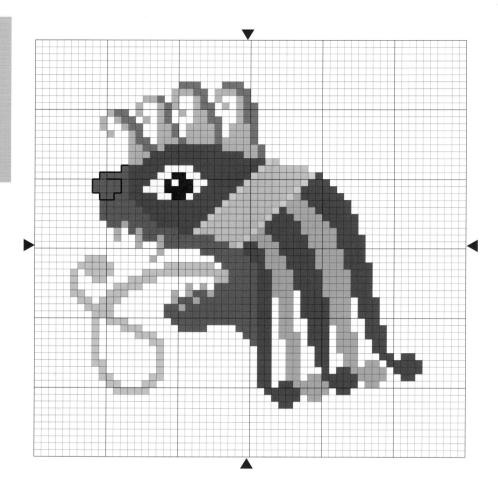

Coaster 6
Thread required

	Anchor Stranded Cotton	Kreinik	Strands for cross stitch	Amount
	403*		2	6.2cm (2⁷⁄₁₆in)
	1		2	7.1cm (2¹³⁄₁₆in)
	101		2	48.9cm (19¼in)
	890		2	6.5cm (2⁹⁄₁₆in)
	298		2	52.7cm (20⅝in)
	1064		2	48.9cm (19¼in)
	1068		2	112.9cm (44⁷⁄₁₆in)
	205		2	15.6cm (6⅛in)
	206		2	25cm (9¹³⁄₁₆in)
		Japan#5	2	7.7cm (3in)

*2 Strands for back stitch

Two Men's Heads Cards

hese are a small part of a larger design in the *Book of Kells* and the expressions on the faces made me laugh, so I had to include them. They are fun to stitch on 16# Hardanger. Add the backstitch after the design is finished and the men will seem to come alive! I thought these dark green cards from Impress were a perfect match for the stitching.

Other ideas for these designs
- cushion centres
- teapot mat
- book cover

1

Design size
6.5 x 12.9cm
(2⁹⁄₁₆ x 5¹⁄₁₆in)

Stitch count
41 x 81

Materials
16# Hardanger

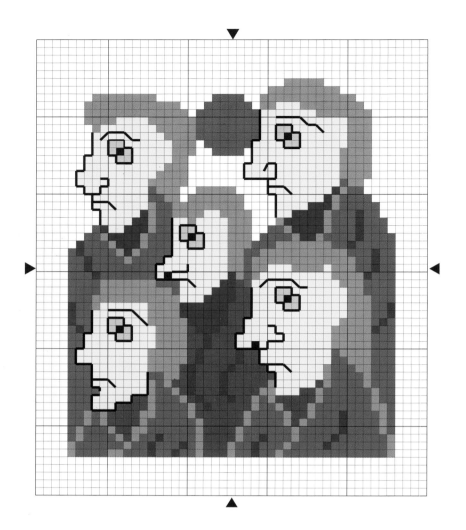

1
Thread required

	Anchor Stranded Cotton	Strands for cross stitch	Amount
	403*	2	28cm (11in)
	890	2	183.5cm (72¼in)
	386/390	2	219.2cm (86⁵⁄₁₆in)
	339	2	195.7cm (77in)
	217	2	60.8cm (23¹⁵⁄₁₆in)
	47	2	23.1cm (9¹⁄₁₆in)
	905	2	27.6cm (10⅞in)
	390	2	13.8cm (5⁷⁄₁₆in)

*1 Strand for back stitch

2

Design size
8.1 x 12.1cm
(3³⁄₁₆ x 4¾in)

Stitch count
51 x 76

Materials
16# Hardanger

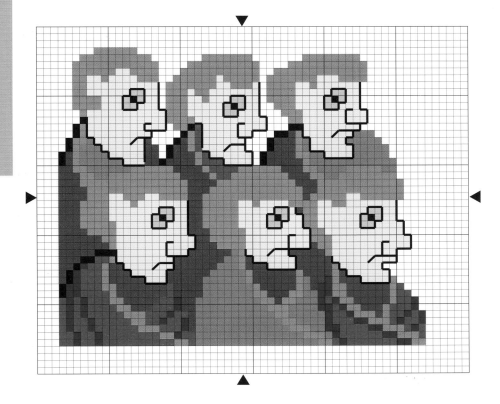

2
Thread required

	Anchor Stranded Cotton	Strands for cross stitch	Amount
	403*	2	46.8cm (18⅜in)
	890	2	220.4cm (86¾in)
	162	2	84.7cm (33⁵⁄₁₆in)
	217	2	95.2cm (37½in)
	400	2	64.8cm (25½in)
	386/390	1	219.6cm (86⁷⁄₁₆in)
	340	2	24.7cm (9⅝in)
	44	2	25.9cm (10³⁄₁₆in)
	390	2	16.2cm (6⅜in)

*1 Strand for back stitch

Three Small Fish

I have made these into a picture and a card by varying the size of the fabric. As the pink fish design is bigger, it is stitched on 22#, whereas the green and blue fish is on 16#. They are taken from letters – the pink design is obviously a 'Q', and the green and blue one could be an 'O'. Fish occurred quite frequently in the earlier manuscripts. When the green and blue one was finished, I thought it would make an unusual card, so I stitched it again during a train journey, and found the dusky-pink card from Impress just right to finish it off. Aperture size: 8 x 10.5cm (3⅛ x 4⅛in).

Other ideas for these designs
- a repetitive border suitable for the bathroom
- lid for a porcelain or wooden pot

Green and blue fish

Design size
7.9 x 7.9cm
(3⅛ x 3⅛in)

Stitch count
50 x 50

Materials
16# Aida

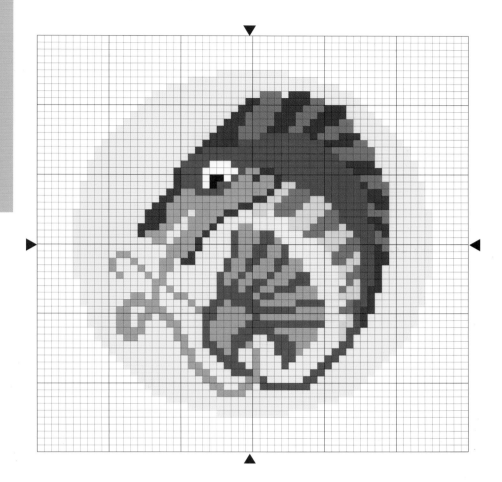

Green and blue fish
Thread required

	Anchor Stranded Cotton	Strands for cross stitch	Amount
	386	2	436.4cm (171¹⁵⁄₁₆in)
	1036	2	56.3cm (22⅛in)
	1034	2	48.2cm (18¹⁵⁄₁₆in)
	1033	2	24.7cm (9¹¹⁄₁₆in)
	1031	2	22.7cm (8¹⁵⁄₁₆in)
	217	2	131.7cm (51¹³⁄₁₆in)
	214	2	46.2cm (18³⁄₁₆in)
	870	2	38.5cm (15⅛in)
	403	2	1.2cm (⁷⁄₁₆in)
	1	2	4.5cm (1¾in)

Pink fish

Design size
5.9 x 7.5cm
(2⁵⁄₁₆ x 2¹⁵⁄₁₆in)

Stitch count
51 x 65

Materials
22# Aida

Pink fish
Thread required

	Anchor Stranded Cotton	Strands for cross stitch	Amount
	969	2	123.5cm (48⅝in)
	968	2	35.4cm (13¹⁵⁄₁₆in)
	972	2	117.9cm (46⅜in)
	873	2	162.7cm (64in)
	873 & 969	1 strand of each	4.1cm (1⅝in)
	972 & 873	1 strand of each	77.5cm (30½in)
	386	2	148.2cm (58⅜in)
	403*	2	2.4cm (¹⁵⁄₁₆in)
	1	2	3.5cm (1⅜in)

*2 Strands for back stitch

Peacock aHD
SalamaHDer Bookmarks

These designs come from the the *Book of Kells*. The peacock is one of many in this book, all with the same surprised expression. The peacock is worked on a ready-made bookmark. These are useful because they do not need any further making-up once the embroidery is complete. The salamander was worked on a 27cm (11⅙in) strip of 14# 55mm (2⅛in) Aida band. I finished the bookmark by ironing a strip of Vilene on to the back, and adding a tassel made from the remaining threads. This design shows the outline of red dots that traditionally occurs on many of the decorated Celtic letters.

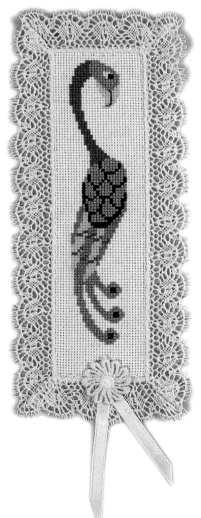

Peacock

Design size
2.8 x 15cm
(1⅛ x 5⅞in)

Stitch count
20 x 106

Materials
18# fabric

Salamander

Design size
3.8 x 19.2cm
(1½ x 7⁹⁄₁₆in)

Stitch count
21 x 106

Materials
14# fabric

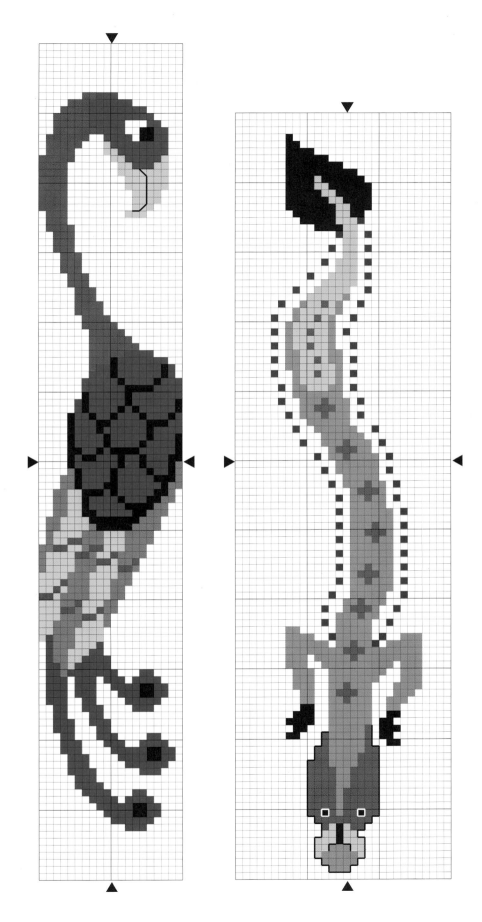

Peacock
Thread required

	Anchor Stranded Cotton	Strands for cross stitch	Amount
■	188	2	174.7cm (68¾in)
■	298	2	56.9cm (22⅜in)
■	970	2	46.8cm (18⅜in)
■	873	2	65.2cm (25¹¹⁄₁₆in)
■	403*	2	44.3cm (17⅞in)
	1	2	2.2cm (⅞in)

*2 Strands for back stitch

Salamander
Thread required

	Anchor Stranded Cotton	Strands for cross stitch	Amount
■	208	2	194.9cm (76¾in)
■	403*	2	66.4cm (26⅛in)
■	298	2	55.6cm (21⅞in)
■	111	2	62.5cm (24⅝in)
■	47	2	28.7cm (11⁵⁄₁₆in)
	1**		1cm (⅜in)

*2 Strands for back stitch (for face) **2 Strands for back stitch (for eye)

Other ideas for these designs
• fingerplate worked on 14#
• spectacles case worked on 18#

Three Animal Pictures

T hese three designs worked on 14# Aida are from the *Book of Kells*. Two of them were from one decorative letter, but I took the liberty of changing the colour of the wolf to make a matching set. Combining two thread colours together gives an 'old' feel to the pictures. The frames shown have an aperture of 12.5 x 17cm (4⅞ x 6¹¹⁄₁₆in).

1

Design size
10.3 x 6.9cm
(4 1/16 x 2 11/16 in)

Stitch count
57 x 38

Materials
14# Aida

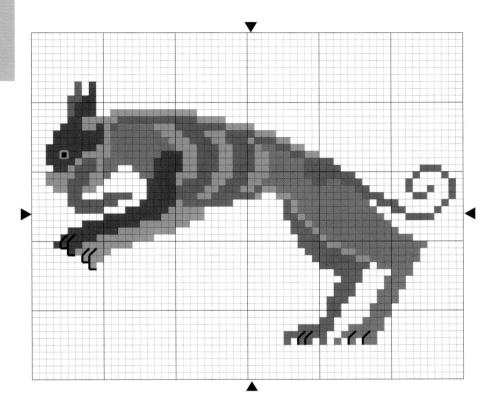

1
Thread required

	Anchor Stranded Cotton	Strands for cross stitch	Amount
	403*	2	3.2cm (1 1/4 in)
	307**	2	88.9cm (35in)
	339	2	50.5cm (19 7/8 in)
	307/339	2	67.1cm (26 3/8 in)
	217	2	54.2cm (21 5/16 in)
	217/307	2	110.2cm (43 3/8 in)

*2 Strands for back stitch **1 Strand for back stitch (for eye)

(1 skein of each of these threads will stitch all three pictures)

2

Design size
11.6 x 5.6cm
(4⁹⁄₁₆ x 2³⁄₁₆in)

Stitch count
64 x 31

Materials
14# Aida

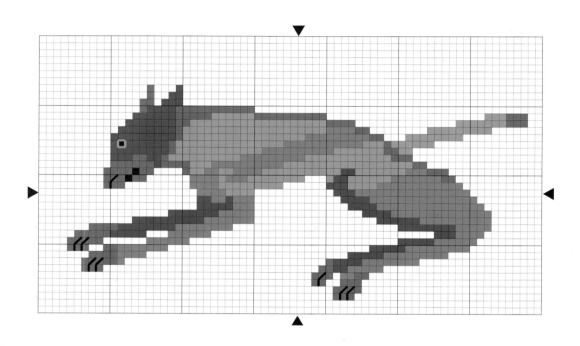

2
Thread required

	Anchor Stranded Cotton	Strands for cross stitch	Amount
	403*	2	3.3cm (1⁵⁄₁₆in)
	307**	2	107.9cm (42in)
	339	2	7.9cm (3⅛in)
	307/339	2	58.3cm (22¹⁵⁄₁₆in)
	217	2	73.6cm (29in)
	217/307	2	123.2cm (48½in)

*2 Strands for back stitch **2 Strands for back stitch (for eye)

3

Design size
12.7 x 6.5cm
(5 x 2⁹⁄₁₆in)

Stitch count
70 x 36

Materials
14# Aida

Other ideas for these designs
- cards
- worked along an Aida band to make a towel border
- pencil case

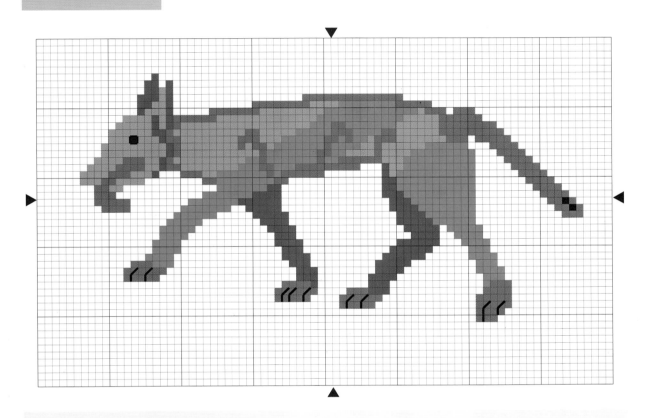

3
Thread required

Anchor Stranded Cotton		Strands for cross stitch	Amount
	403*	2	4.1cm (1⅝in)
	307	2	109.3cm (43in)
	339	2	40.7cm (16in)
	307/339	2	88.9cm (35in)
	217	2	70.8cm (27⅞in)
	217/307	2	146.3cm (57⁹⁄₁₆in)

*2 Strands for back stitch

Lion and Eagle Cards

This lion symbol comes from the *Book of Durrow*. It is worked on pale grey 28# Jobelan over 2 threads. It fits a 24.1 x 34.3cm (9½ x 13½in) rectangular aperture to make an attractive card. The eagle also came from the *Book of Durrow*. It is the eagle symbol of St. John. Worked on 16# Aida, it is set into a dark green Impress card. You'll need an aperture that is 8 x 10.5cm (3⅛ x 4⅛in).

Lion

Design size
12.2 x 8.9cm
(4¹³⁄₁₆ x 3½in)

Stitch count
67 x 49

Materials
28# Jobelan

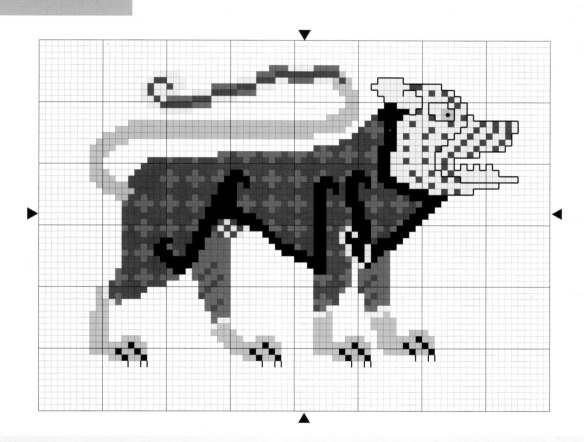

Lion
Thread required

	Anchor Stranded Cotton	Strands for cross stitch	Amount
⬛	403*	2	139.6cm (55in)
	298	2	143.1cm (56⁵⁄₁₆in)
	266	2	138.5cm (54½in)
	340	2	243.6cm (95⅝in)
	386	2	131.5cm (51¾in)

*2 Strands for back stitch and 2 for French knot

Eagle

Design size
6.4 x 14.8cm
(2½ x 5¹³⁄₁₆in)

Materials
16# Aida

Stitch count
40 x 60

Other ideas for the lion and the eagle
- small pictures with a border
- lid for a box
- pincushion worked in wool on canvas

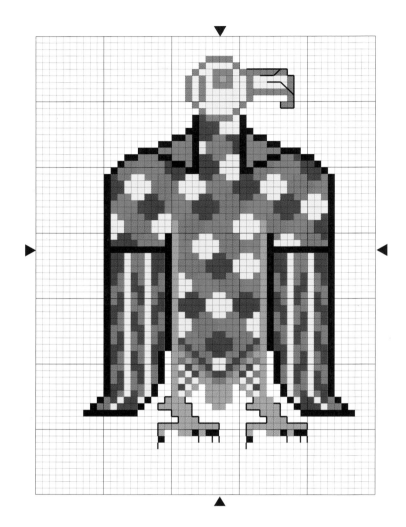

Eagle
Thread required

	Anchor Stranded Cotton	Strands for cross stitch	Amount
	403*	2	98.5cm (38¾in)
	386	2	128.4cm (50⁹⁄₁₆in)
	336	2	57.9cm (22¹³⁄₁₆in)
	338	2	136.9cm (53⅞in)
	341	2	126.8cm (49¹⁵⁄₁₆in)
	215	2	85.1cm (33½in)

*2 Strands for back stitch

paperweight fish

This can be worked quickly on 18# Aida and makes a delightful present. The colours are the same as those in the illuminated letter 'T' (see page 99), so you could stitch it to make use of those left-over threads. It is shown here in a plain glass paperweight with an aperture of 5cm (approx. 2in).

Design size
4 x 4cm (1⁹⁄₁₆ x 1⁹⁄₁₆in)

Stitch count
28 x 28

Materials
18# Aida

Thread required

	Anchor Stranded Cotton	Strands for cross stitch	Amount
	236	2	56.2cm (22⅛in)
	337	2	21.6cm (8½in)
	338	2	17.3cm (6¹³⁄₁₆in)
	341	2	45.7cm (18in)
	386	2	65.5cm (25¹³⁄₁₆in)
	232	2	15.5cm (6⅛in)

Other ideas for this design

- small round card
- gift tag on 22#
- herb sac

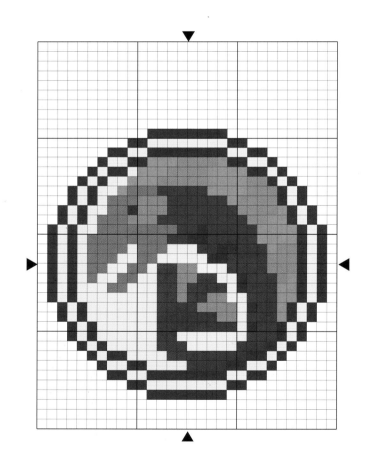

Towel Borders

The starting point for these designs was a border from Folio 67 of the *Book of Kells*. It is worked on a white 75mm (3in) Aida band. When I found the luxurious dark green towel, I thought it was perfect for the cock and hens design. At the same time I bought a matching facecloth and sewed into one corner one of the designs worked on to a small circle of 22# Aida.

When I bought the green towel, I noticed a beautiful dark blue one which seemed just right for the animal design. The animals came from the Gunderstrup Cauldron and, as this is made of metal, I chose to do the animals in the matching blues and greens, so that the towels became a pair. The animals needed something in the middle where they met, so I put in a small motif that will come in useful for other things.

Cock and hens

Design size
46.1 x 6.7cm
(18 1/8 x 2 5/8in)

Stitch count
254 x 37

Materials
14# Aida

Cock and hens
Thread required

	Anchor Stranded Cotton	Strands for cross stitch	Amount
	403*	2	114.7cm (45 1/8in)
	215	2	215.3cm (84 3/4in)
	217	2	270.4cm (106 7/16in)
	890	2	286.2cm (112 11/16in)
	127	2	213.5cm (84in)
	175	2	82.9cm (32 5/8in)
	386	2	135.7cm (53 7/16in)

*2 Strands for back stitch and 2 for French knot

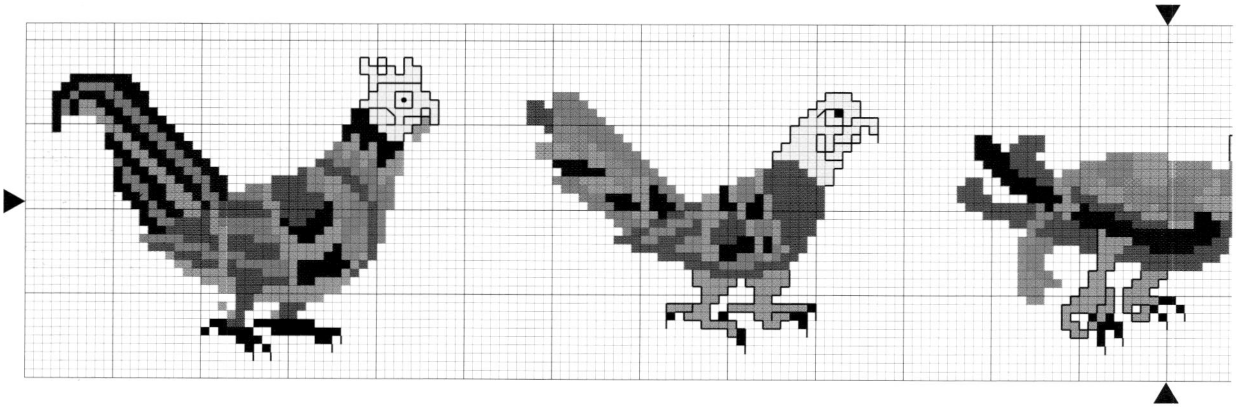

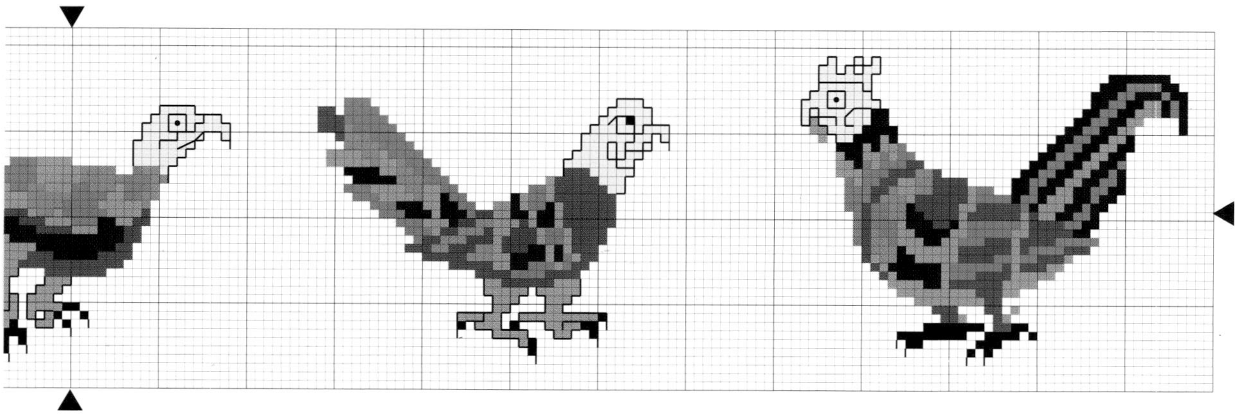

Animals

Design size
44.5 x 7.3cm
(17½ x 2⅞in)

Stitch count
245 x 40

Materials
14# Aida

Animals
Thread required

	Anchor Stranded Cotton	Strands for cross stitch	Amount
	403*	2	72.1cm (28⅜in)
	215	2	314cm (123⅜in)
	217	2	261.2cm (102¹³⁄₁₆in)
	890	2	163cm (64³⁄₁₆in)
	127	2	263cm (103³⁄₁₆in)
	123	2	348.7cm (137⁵⁄₁₆in)
	386	2	71.8cm (28¼in)

*2 Strands for back stitch

Other ideas for these designs
- single hen or animal as a card
- tea towel borders
- cushion centres
- a bell pull with the pictures worked vertically, and a border added between each one

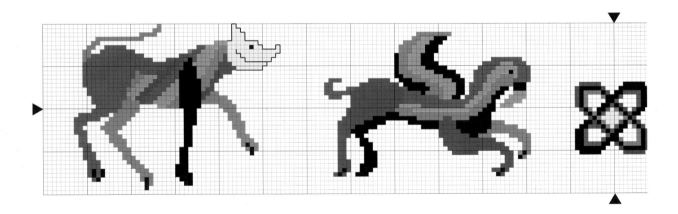

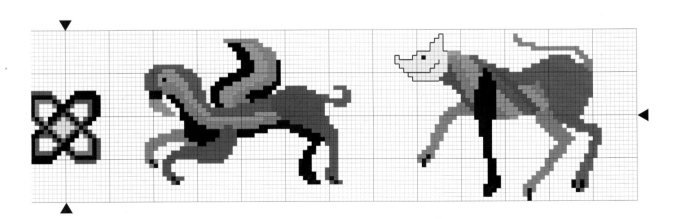

Stanwick Man

This design was taken from a bronze horse-head mount found near Stanwick in Yorkshire. I have used a combination of greens and blues to give a rich colouring which is intensified by the silver line round the aperture of the card. It was stitched on 16# Hardanger.

Design size
7 x 10.2cm
(2¾ x 4in)

Stitch count
44 x 64

Materials
16# Hardanger

Thread required

	Anchor Stranded Cotton	Strands for cross stitch	Amount
■	403	2	120.7cm (47½in)
■	1066/1062	2	126.4cm (49¾in)
■	1068	2	213.1cm (83⅞in)
■	216	2	106.2cm (41¹³⁄₁₆in)
■	1066/216	2	89.9cm (35⅜in)
■	1096	2	63.2cm (24⅞in)

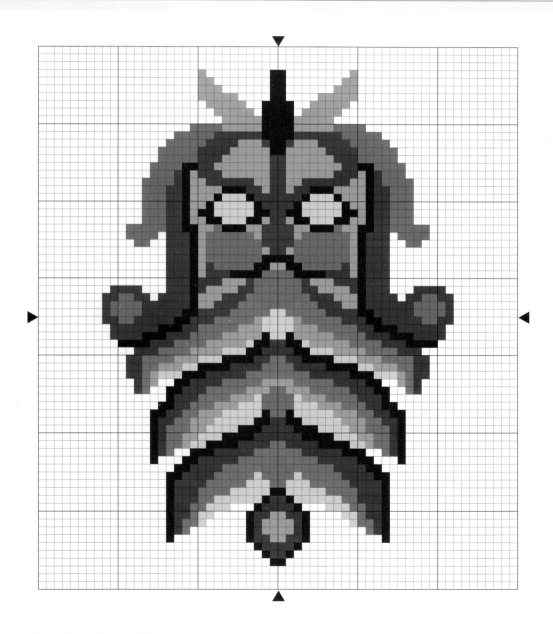

Other ideas for 'Stanwick man'
• a notebook holder on 22# fabric

• coasters

Torque head

This design was inspired by a torque (a twisted metal necklace or collar) from France. It is worked on 22# fabric, but does not take very long because it is only small. It would make a lovely present.

Design size
4.7 x 6.9cm
(1⅞ x 2¾in)

Stitch count
41 x 60

Materials
22# fabric

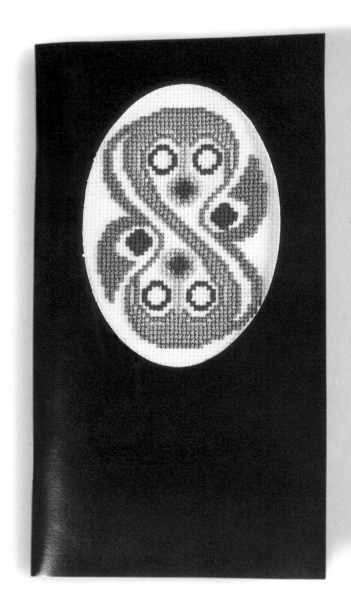

Thread required

	Anchor Stranded Cotton	Strands for cross stitch	Amount
	70	2	40.1cm (15¾in)
	970	2	173.3cm (68¼in)
	968	2	45.4cm (17⅞in)
	969	2	91.9cm (36³⁄₁₆in)

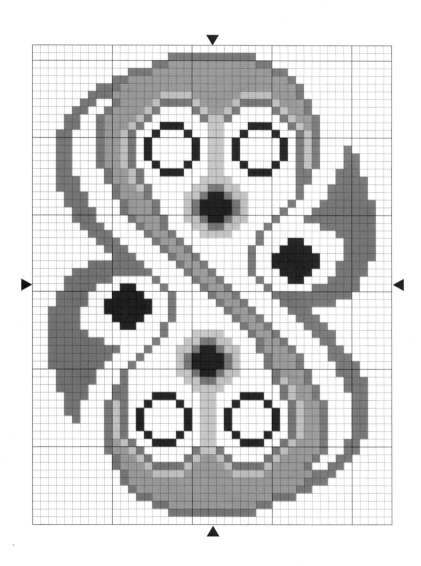

Other ideas for the 'torque head'

- any small item with an oval aperture
- spectacles case

6
ILLUMINATED LETTERS

Illuminated manuscripts in Great Britain are thought to date from the time of Saint Columba. They were copies of the four Gospels and they helped travelling monks to spread the Christian message. Originally it was just the initial letters that were decorated, but later the scribes of the *Book of Durrow* and then the *Book of Kells* and the *Lindisfarne Gospels* created 'carpet pages'. Some were planned geometrically with compasses and rulers, and then filled in with patterns so that every possible space appears to have been used. Spirals and plaits are intertwined with stylized animals and birds with elongated bodies and tails, and they have the most expressive faces. You see something new each time you look at them. It must have been painstakingly slow work; it is estimated that it may have taken up to thirty years to produce the *Book of Kells*.

The colours used were mainly yellow, red, dark brown and green. Blue was a later addition, but it was limited because it came from lapis lazuli and had to be imported from Arab countries, which made it expensive. Often the initials were enhanced by an outline of red dots. I have kept the typical colouring in many of the designs in the book, but I have changed it where it is more appropriate for today.

The book includes two alphabets of letters taken from the manuscripts, but as the Latin gospels didn't include every letter, I have devised one of each in the same style so that there is a complete alphabet. These letters can be very useful for personalizing cards and gifts.

There is also a challenge in the form of a large sampler design of Celtic letters, each individual letter being decorated with creatures from the *Book of Kells* and the *Lindisfarne Gospels*.

Illuminated 'T'

ome of the manuscripts are really beautiful works of art. To create something as detailed and fine in stitching, they would need to be massive, but they would still not be as good. I did, however, want to use at least one decorated letter in the book. I reached a compromise by taking the shape of the 'T', stitching it on 28# Jobelan over 2 threads then filling it with stitched patterns inspired by sections of the manuscripts. I chose colours that would fit into most colour schemes. As you stitch this, you will notice that there are even small fish designs tucked into the decoration. I really enjoyed stitching this, and was pleased with the end result.

Design size
22 x 23.6cm
(8¹¹⁄₁₆ x 9⁵⁄₁₆in)

Stitch count
121 x 130

Materials
28# Jobelan

Thread required

	Anchor Stranded Cotton	Strands for cross stitch	Amount
	236	2	560.8cm (220 13/16in)
	337	2	292.2cm (115in)
	338	2	97.2cm (38 1/4in)
	339	2	105.6cm (41 9/16in)
	341	2	344.1cm (135 7/16in)
	235	2	295.9cm (116 1/2in)
	779	2	298.2cm (117 3/8in)
	386	2	876.1cm (344 7/8in)
	232	2	132.4cm (52 1/8in)

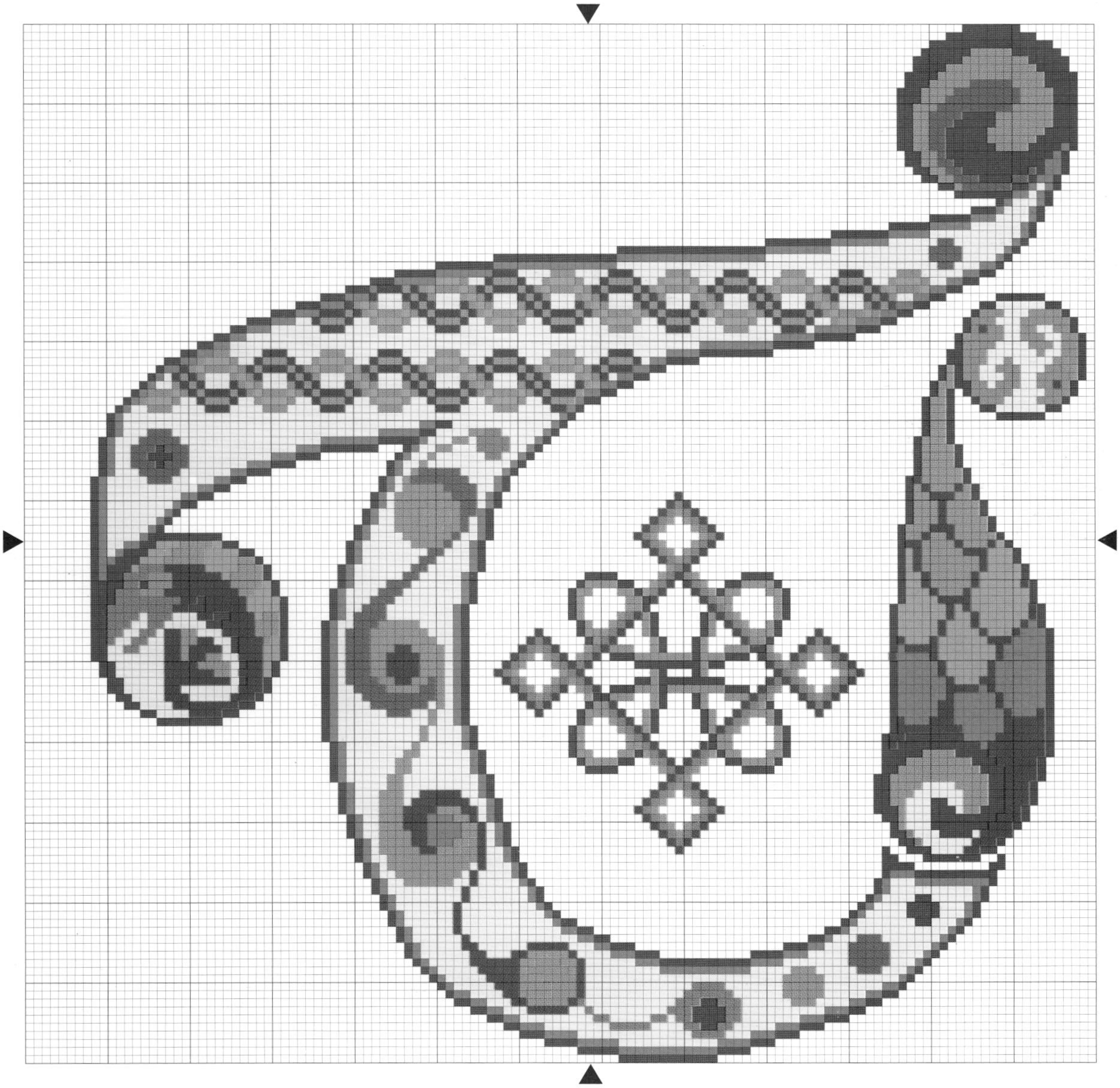

Zoomorphic Sampler

This is a challenging project, but the end result is well worth the effort. As every letter is decorated, each one can be used independently, which is useful for personalizing cards and gifts. It was worked on 16# Aida.

Design size
46.7 x 37.8cm
(18⅜ x 14⅞in)

Stitch count
294 x 238

Materials
16# Aida

Thread required

	Anchor Stranded Cotton	Kreinik	Strands for cross stitch	Amount
▰	403*		2	2489.1cm (980in)
	1**		2	24.2cm (9½in)
▰	266		2	2127.6cm (837⅝in)
▰	298		2	813.6cm (320⅛in)
▰	46		2	445.7cm (175⅝in)
▰	340		2	1372.7cm (540⅛in)
▰		Japan#5	2	796.2cm (313⅜in)

*1 Strand for back stitch (for head) **2 Strands for back stitch (for eyes)

A black and white chart which can be enlarged on a photocopier for easier working can be found on page 182.

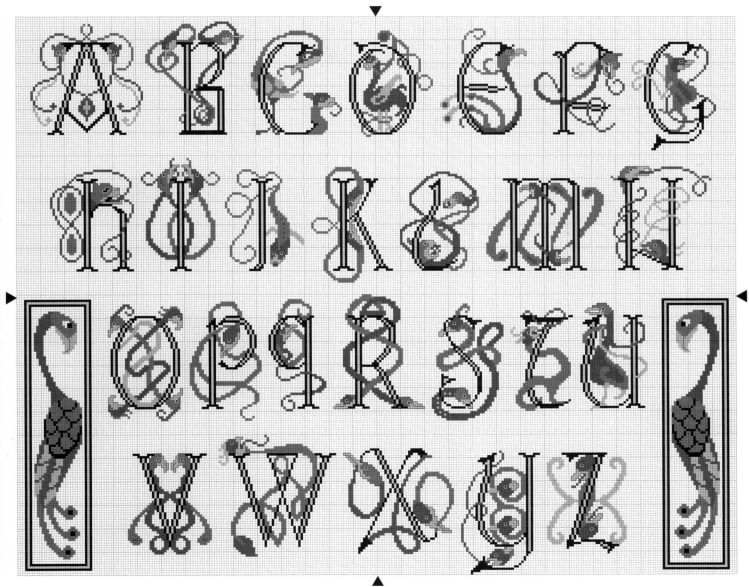

LETTER 'α'

his small design makes an unusual card. Any of the letters given in the large alphabet on page 105 will fit the design.

Design size
7.5 x 9.1cm
(3 x 3⅟₁₆in)

Stitch count
56 x 68

Materials
19# Easistitch

Thread required

	Anchor Stranded Cotton	Strands for cross stitch	Amount
	208	2	53.9cm (21¼in)
	217	2	25.6cm (10⅛in)
	236	2	94.2cm (37¹⁄₁₆in)
	235	2	86cm (33⅞in)
	232	2	90.1cm (35⁷⁄₁₆in)
	335	2	43.7cm (17³⁄₁₆in)

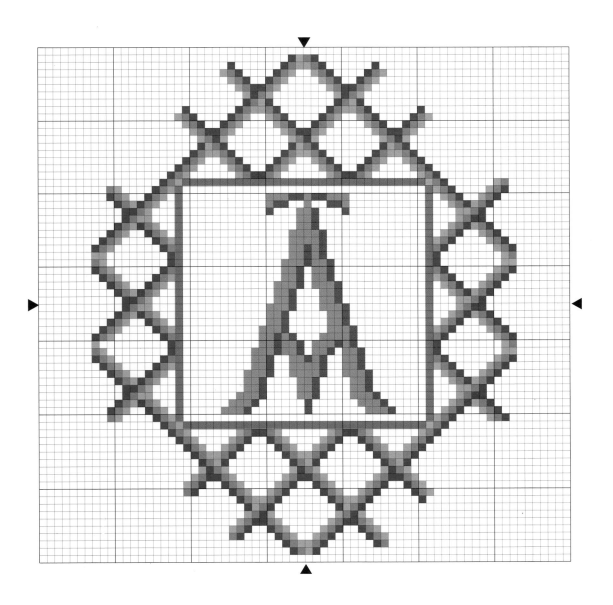

Small Alphabet

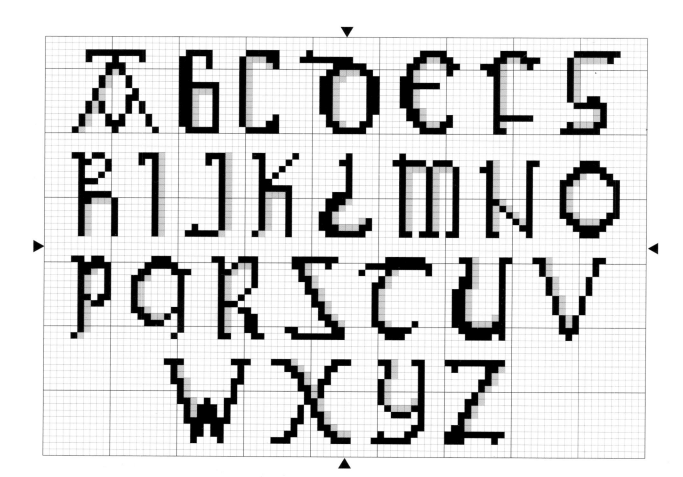

Large Alphabet

7

Borders and Corners

There are many times when a border or a corner is either a practical or decorative addition to a stitched project. Adding a border to a small design can make it into a substantial picture.

Throughout the designs found on Celtic artefacts and in the manuscripts there are numerous patterns that can make wonderful borders. I decided to put together a collection of these to give a source of 'ready-made' borders that can either be used as they are or adapted for your stitched projects.

Some of these are geometric designs which vary in depth and in the repeat length; others are sections of designs that I have made into a border. Wherever possible, I have given the source of the original inspiration, which I hope will be of interest to you.

As many of these designs were adaptations from metal artefacts, I have been able to let my imagination run amok with the colouring. Changing the colours gives a completely new look to the stitching, as I have described in the section on adapting designs on page 4.

I hope you find these helpful in planning your stitching.

Two Borders for a Tote Bag

These are to match the pocket design on page 36. They are worked on strips of 28# Jobelan over 2 threads, then fastened on to the bag. They were based on designs found on helmets and flagons.

1

Design size
13.6 x 5.3cm
(5⁵⁄₁₆ x 2¹⁄₁₆in)

Stitch count
65 x 20

Materials
28# Jobelan,
worked over
2 threads

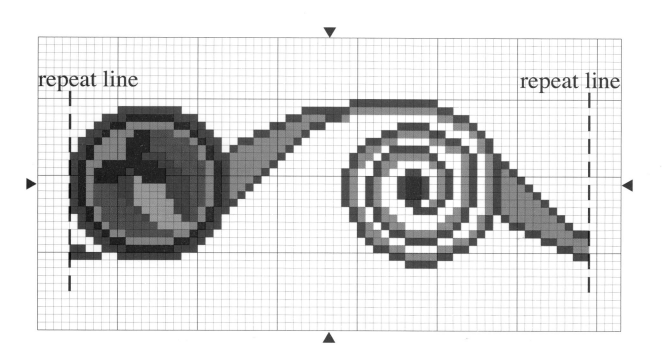

Thread required

	Anchor Stranded Cotton	Strands for cross stitch	Amount
	403	2	49.9cm (19⅝in)
	189	2	132.4cm (52⅛in)
	186	2	113cm (44½in)
	69	2	30.6cm (12in)
	66	2	12cm (4¾in)

2

Design size
13.1 x 6cm
(5⅛ x 2⅜in)

Stitch count
64 x 24

Materials
28# Jobelan

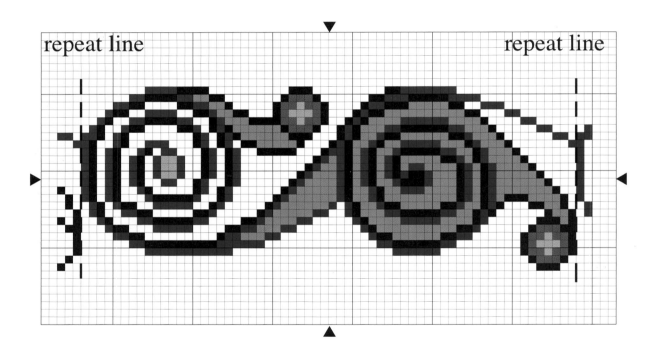

repeat line   repeat line

Thread required

	Anchor Stranded Cotton	Strands for cross stitch	Amount
	403	2	154.5cm (60¹³⁄₁₆in)
	189	2	136.1cm (53⅝in)
	186	2	115.8cm (45⅝in)
	69	2	14.8cm (5¹³⁄₁₆in)
	66	2	7.4cm (2⅞in)

Duvet Cover and Pillow Bands

his design came from a French helmet. It matches the damask cushion and lavender sac on page 44. Each of the duvet corners has a 1m (39⅜in) strip of 75mm (3in) cream Aida band from Fabric Flair, and the pillow design is worked on a 55mm (2in) cream Aida band. I left 28 stitches between each pattern on the duvet cover.

Design size
12.9 x 7.1cm
(5 x 2¹³⁄₁₆in) on 14#

Stitch count
71 x 39
Duvet: leave 28 squares between each pattern

Materials
Duvet
75mm (3in) cream Aida band from Fabric Flair, 1m (39⅜in) for each corner
Pillow
55m (2in) cream Aida band

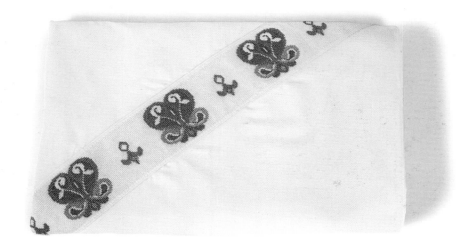

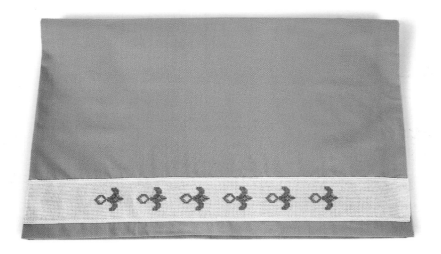

Thread required (for one repeat)

	Anchor Stranded Cotton	Strands for cross stitch	Amount
	896	2	222.3cm (87½in)
	895	2	111.6cm (43¹⁵⁄₁₆in)
	216	2	208.4cm (82in)
	386	2	116.7cm (45¹⁵⁄₁₆in)

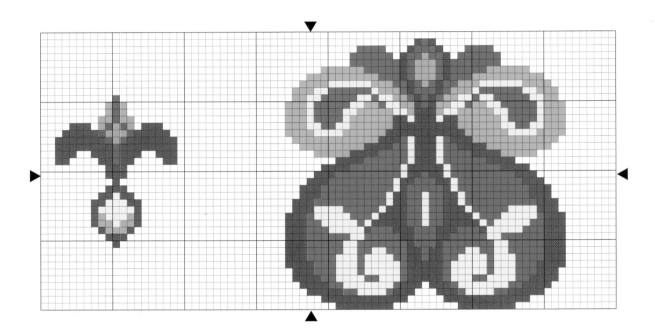

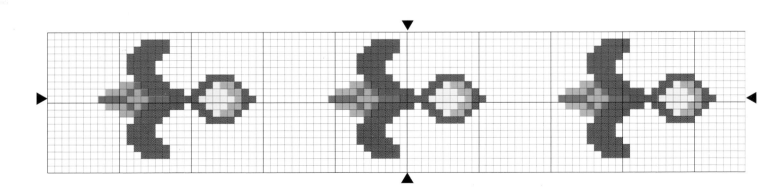

Corner Sampler

his is worked on coffee 28# Jobelan over 2 threads. As well as being interesting as it is, it also gives five designs that can be used independently for other items. It would make a great picture or a striking design to go under a glass-topped table.

Design size
43.9 x 25.9cm
(17⁵⁄₁₆ x 10³⁄₁₆in)

Stitch count
242 x 143

Materials
28# Jobelan

Thread required

	Anchor Stranded Cotton	Strands for cross stitch	Amount
	403	2	328.3cm (129¼in)
	1	2	566.8cm (223⅛in)
	217	2	683cm (268⅞in)
	123	2	621cm (244½in)
	122	2	216.2cm (85⅛in)
	214	2	148.2cm (58⅜in)

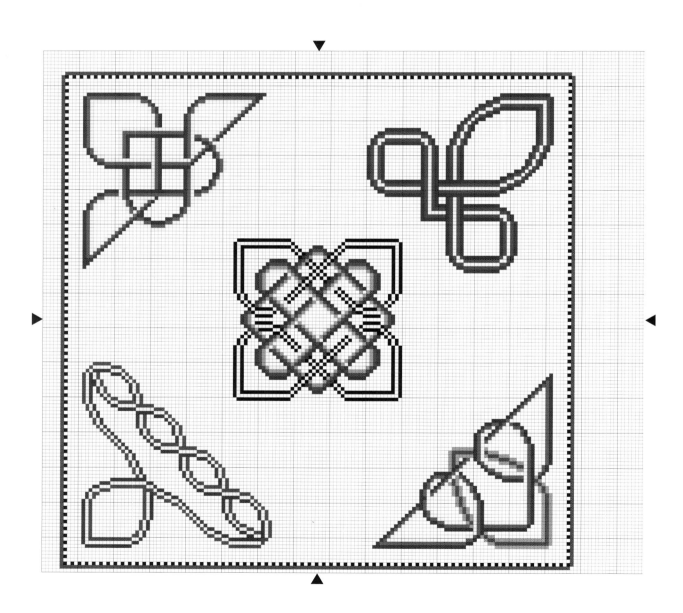

Lemon Towel Border

I took part of this design from the centre of a decorated letter. It is worked on the border of a ready-to-stitch towel, but could be worked on 14# and stitched on to the towel afterwards.

Design size
33.9 x 8.2cm
(13⁵⁄₁₆ x 3³⁄₁₆in)

Stitch count
187 x 45

Materials
14# border fabric

Thread required

	Anchor Stranded Cotton	Strands for cross stitch	Amount
	338	2	237.5cm (93½in)
	341	2	257cm (101³⁄₁₆in)
	398	2	126cm (49⅝in)
	400	2	142.6cm (56⅛in)
	217	2	171.3cm (67⁷⁄₁₆in)

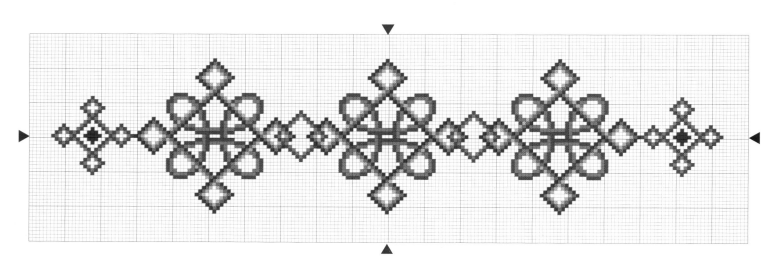

Two Cream Towel Borders

These towels were from my local supermarket, but now look like designer towels with the addition of the borders. They were worked on a 75mm (3in) cream Aida band which was then stitched on to the towels. The colours match the pair of finger plates on page 13.

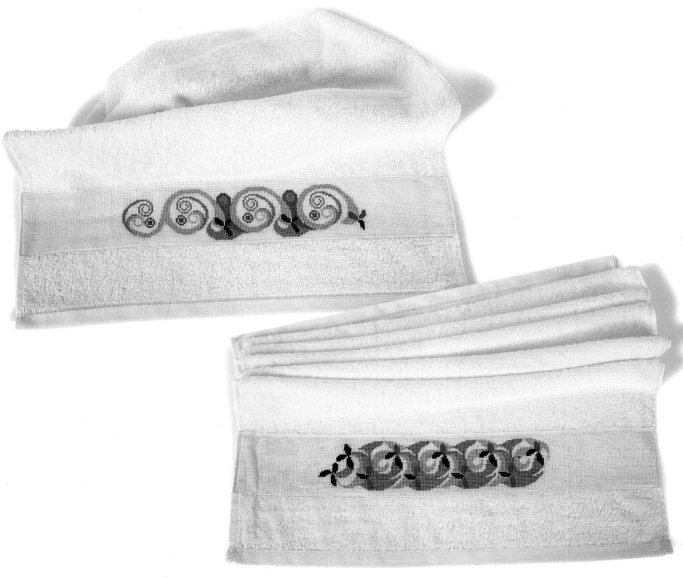

1

Design size
5.7 x 25.7cm
(2¼ x 10⅛in)

Stitch count
36 x 162

Materials
75mm (3in) cream
16# Aida band

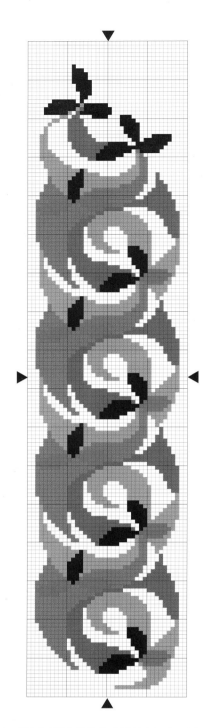

Thread required

	Anchor Stranded Cotton	Strands for cross stitch	Amount
	403	2	206.2cm (81³⁄₁₆in)
	1086	2	121.6cm (47⅞in)
	1027	2	376.8cm (148⁵⁄₁₆in)
	894	2	466.8cm (183¾in)
	779	2	333.9cm (131⁷⁄₁₆in)

2

Design size
5.7 x 26cm
(2¼ x 10¼in)

Stitch count
36 x 164

Materials
75mm (3in) cream
16# Aida band

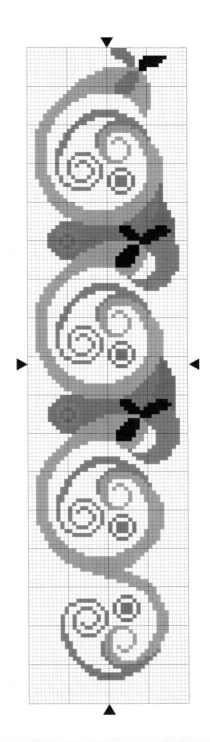

Thread required

	Anchor Stranded Cotton	Strands for cross stitch	Amount
	403	2	58.8cm (23⅛in)
	1086	2	163.3cm (64⅝in)
	1027	2	272.3cm (107⅜in)
	894	2	539.3cm (212⅝in)
	779	2	41.3cm (16¼in)

White Towel Border

This is a small design from an enamelled bronze brooch. It reminds me of a seahorse. Although I worked it on a ready-made towel it could be stitched on a white 75mm (3in) Aida band then fastened to a white towel. I started in the centre and worked outwards, leaving 10 stitches between each pattern.

Design size
3.6 x 7.3cm
(1⅜ x 2⅞in)

Stitch count
20 x 40

Materials
75mm (3in) Aida border 14#

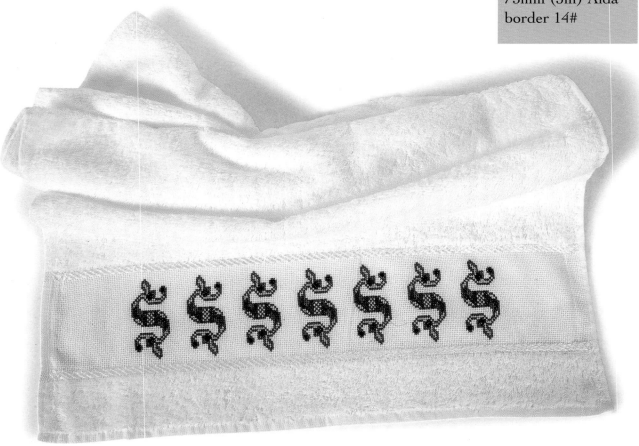

Thread required

	Anchor Stranded Cotton	Strands for cross stitch	Amount
■	403	2	7.4cm (2⅞in)
■	149	2	38cm (15in)
■	189	2	93.5cm (36¹³⁄₁₆in)
■	167	2	38cm (15in)

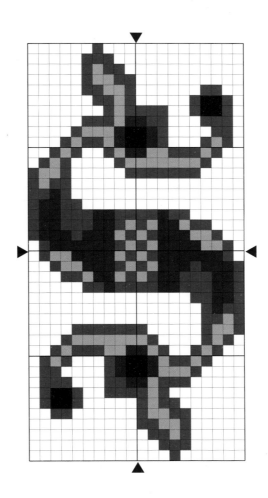

Pink Picture Frame

This was worked on 28# Jobelan over 2 threads. It makes a photograph very special. I chose the colours to match the colours of the flowers in the bouquet, but these could be changed. This frame would also be suitable for an anniversary photograph, perhaps worked in yellows and greens for a Golden Wedding, or dark reds for a Ruby Wedding. The aperture is 16 x 19cm (6⅝₁₆ x 7½in).

Design size
10.7 x 12.5cm
(4³⁄₁₆ x 4⅞in)

Stitch count
59 x 69

Materials
28# Jobelan, worked over 2 threads

Thread required

	Anchor Stranded Cotton	Strands for cross stitch	Amount
	895	2	142.6cm (56⅛in)
	897	2	140.8cm (55⅞in)
	892	2	133.4cm (52½in)

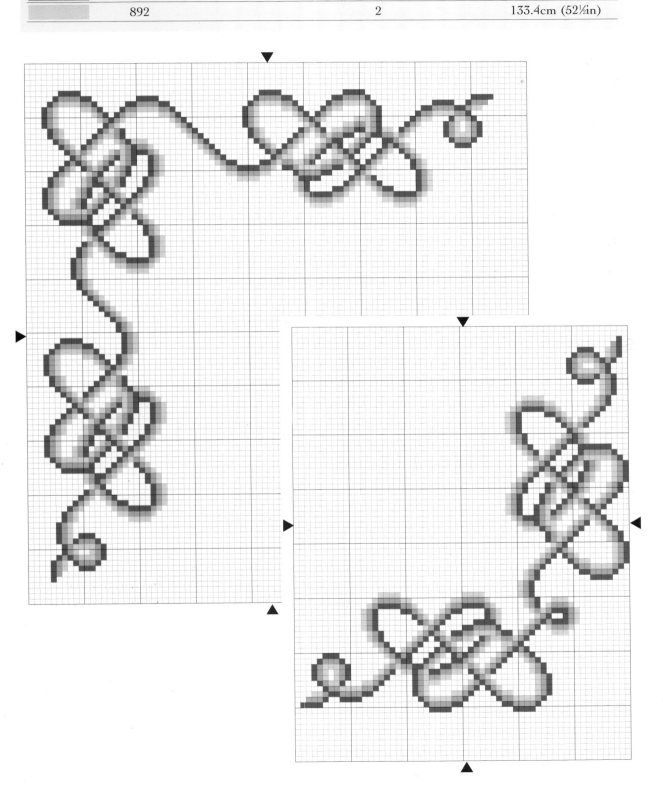

Blue Picture Frame

This is not as delicate as the pink frame, but is also worked on 28# Jobelan over 2 threads. The aperture is 16 x 19cm (6⁵⁄₁₆ x 7½in). It is just right for a graduation or school photograph.

Design size
7.3 x 7.3cm
(2⅞ x 2⅞in)

Stitch count
40 x 40

Materials
28# Jobelan,
worked over
2 threads

Thread required

	Anchor Stranded Cotton	Strands for cross stitch	Amount
	133	2	96.3cm (37⅞in)
	397	2	102.3cm (40⁵⁄₁₆in)
	127	2	103.3cm (40¹¹⁄₁₆in)

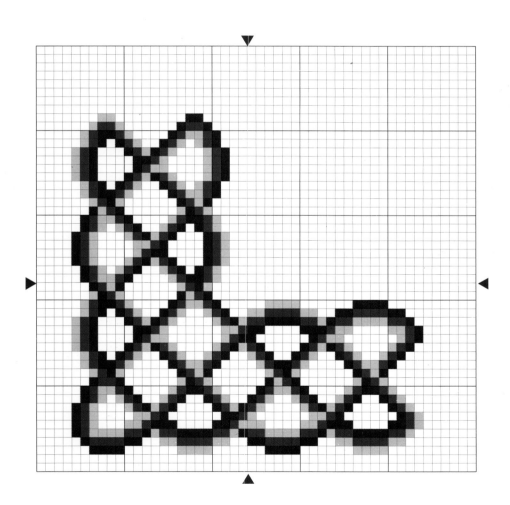

Dinner Mat, Bread Basket Cloth, Napkin Corner and Matching Coasters

The dinner mat was worked on denim-blue 28# Jobelan over 2 threads, and then the edges were frayed. The mat is 45 x 35cm (17¹¹⁄₁₆ x 13¾in). Work the design 4cm (1⁹⁄₁₆in) up and 4cm (1⁹⁄₁₆in) across then fray 2cm (¾in) down each side. The bread basket cloth and napkin corner were worked on Jobelan to match the dinner mat. The basket cloth is on denim-blue, and the napkin on white. I added a narrow lace edging to make them more striking. They are both 37 x 37cm (14⁹⁄₁₆ x 14⁹⁄₁₆in). The coasters were worked on the same fabric then made up using deep coasters with an aperture of 8.5 x 8.5cm (3⁵⁄₁₆ x 3⁵⁄₁₆in).

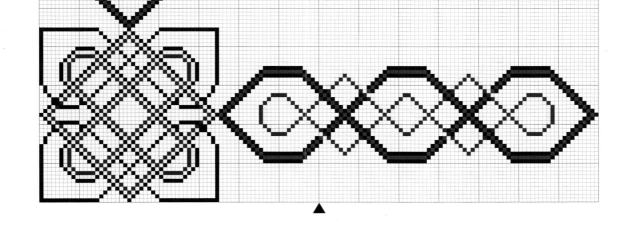

Dinner Mat

Design size
25.4 x 25.4cm
(10 x 10in)

Stitch count
140 x 140

Materials
Denim-blue
Jobelan 28#,
worked over
2 threads

Thread required

Anchor Stranded Cotton	Strands for cross stitch	Amount
127	2	528.3cm (208in)
1	2	226.9cm (89⁵⁄₁₆in)
44	2	221.3cm (87⅛in)
147	2	166.7cm (65⅝in)

Bread Basket Cloth

Design size
3.8 x 3.8cm
(1½ x 1½in)

Stitch count
21 x 21

Materials
Denim-blue Jobelan 28#, worked over 2 threads

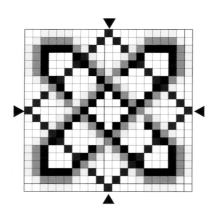

Threads required

	Anchor Stranded Cotton	Strands for cross stitch	Amount
	1	2	38.9cm (15⁵⁄₁₆in)
	117	2	35.2cm (13⅞in)
	127	2	31.5cm (12⅜in)
	44	2	16.7cm (6⁹⁄₁₆in)

Napkin

Design size
3.8 x 3.8cm
(1½ x 1½in)

Stitch count
21 x 21

Materials
White Jobelan 28#, worked over 2 threads

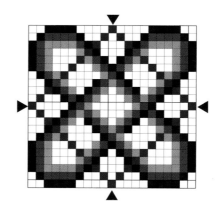

Threads required

	Anchor Stranded Cotton	Strands for cross stitch	Amount
	127	2	38.9cm (15⁵⁄₁₆in)
	147	2	35.2cm (13⅞in)
	117	2	31.5cm (12⅜in)
	44	2	16.7cm (6⁹⁄₁₆in)

Coasters

Design size
8.2 x 8.2cm
(3³⁄₁₆ x 3³⁄₁₆in)

Stitch count
45 x 45

Materials
Denim-blue
Jobelan 28#,
worked over
2 threads

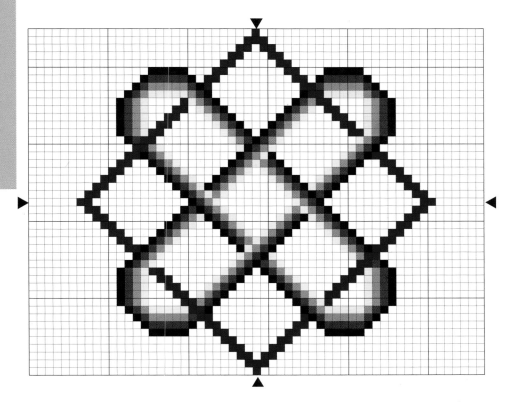

Threads required

	Anchor Stranded cotton	Strands for cross stitch	Amount
	1	2	53.7cm (21⅛in)
	117	2	57.4cm (22⅗in)
	147	2	61.1cm (24⅛in)
	127	2	64.8cm (25½in)
	44	2	72.2cm (28⁷⁄₁₆in)

matchihg Fihger plate aho Light Switch Border

s light switches are often near doors, I thought that it would be nice to have a pair of matching designs. The finger plate is worked on a strip of 22# Hardanger, and the light switch on 14# Aida. I worked the light switch design on a square piece of fabric, then ironed Vilene on the back to stop it fraying and make it stiffer, and then I used the template with the plastic switch cover to cut it out. The finger plates also look better for having a piece of Vilene on the back. The plastic finger plates and switch covers are readily available.

Finger Plate

Design size
3.3 x 17.8 cm
(1⁵⁄₁₆ x 7in)

Stitch count
29 x 154

Materials
55mm (2⅛in) band
of 22# Hardanger

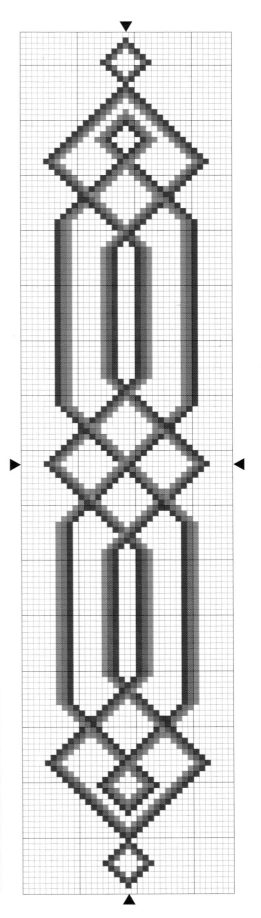

Thread required

	Anchor Stranded Cotton	Strands for cross stitch	Amount
	121	2	74.8cm (29⅜in)
	122	2	76cm (29⅞in)
	123	2	86cm (33¹³⁄₁₆in)
	204	2	70.7cm (27¹³⁄₁₆in)
	205	2	77.5cm (30½in)
	230	2	70.7cm (27¹³⁄₁₆in)

(1 skein of each of these threads is enough to stitch both designs)

Light Switch Border

Design size
13.6 x 13.6cm
(5⅜ x 5⅜in)

Stitch count
75 x 75

Materials
14# Aida

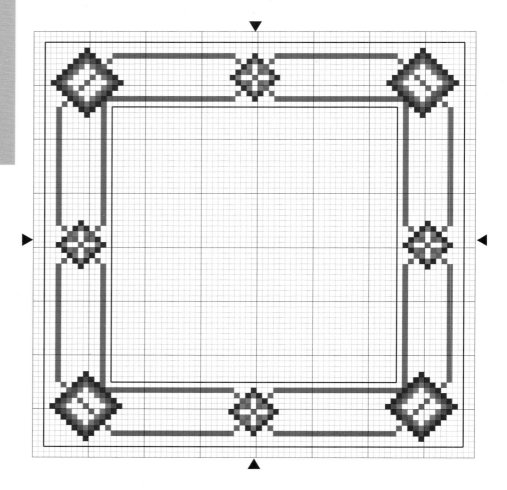

Thread required

	Anchor Stranded Cotton	Strands for cross stitch	Amount
	121	2	50cm (19¹¹⁄₁₆in)
	122	2	37cm (14⅝in)
	123	2	68.5cm (27in)
	205	2	200cm (78¾in)

Aida Pincushion

This is a simple but effective design to work in shades of turquoise on 28# Jobelan stitched over 2 threads. The pattern came from the *Book of Durrow*. I added a bought tassel which makes the pincushion easier to pick up when it is full of pins. When the design was complete, I ironed Vilene on the back before cutting out the octagon.

Design size
10.3 x 10.3cm
(4 x 4in)

Stitch count
57 x 57

Materials
28# Jobelan,
worked over
2 threads

Thread required

	Anchor Stranded Cotton	Strands for cross stitch	Amount
	1092	2	196.3cm (77 5/16in)
	186	2	194.5cm (76 9/16in)
	188	2	190.8cm (75 1/8in)

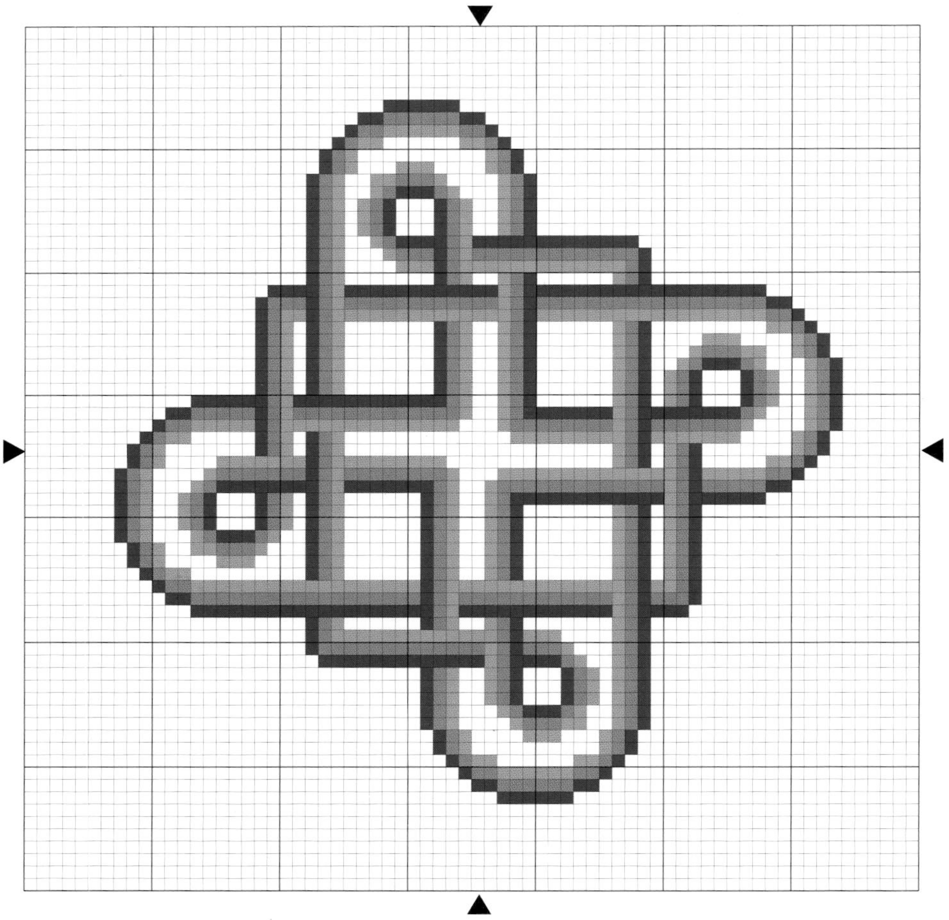

Bookmark

This was inspired by carvings on stone crosses, so it seemed appropriate to make the design into the shape of a cross. It was worked on 14# fabric and as it is only small you could use up threads left from other projects. I fastened a tassel at the top, not at the bottom, so that the book can still be stood upright.

Design size
8.2 x 17.4cm
(3³⁄₁₆ x 6¹³⁄₁₆in)

Stitch count
45 x 96

Materials
14# fabric

Thread required

	Anchor Stranded Cotton	Strands for cross stitch	Amount
	397	2	87.1cm (34⁵⁄₁₆in)
	1076	2	113.9cm (44¹³⁄₁₆in)
	1068	2	42.6cm (16¾in)
	127	2	122.7cm (48⅝in)
	851	2	48.2cm (18¹⁵⁄₁₆in)

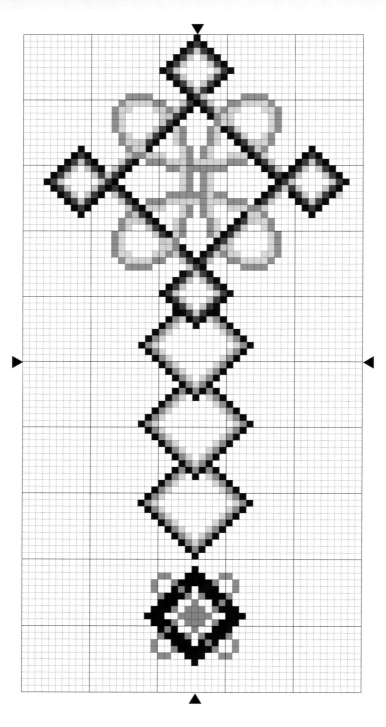

Three Borders for a Red Bolster Cushion

This is a super cushion with three borders worked in bright colours. It makes a striking pair with the green cushion. The two smaller designs are repetitive geometric cross patterns, but the larger one in the middle is a palmette (palm leaf) pattern taken from a torque.

Design 1

Design size
7.3 x 7.8cm
(2⅞ x 3¹⁄₁₆in)

Stitch count
40 x 43

Materials
28# Jobelan,
worked over
2 threads

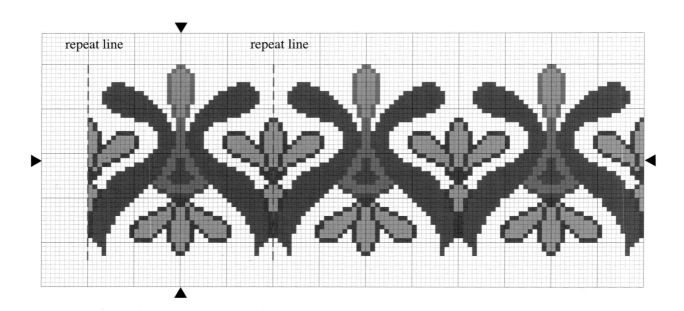

repeat line   repeat line

Thread required (for one repeat)

	Anchor Stranded Cotton	Strands for cross stitch	Amount
	896	2	266.3cm (104¹³⁄₁₆in)
	117	2	16.7cm (6⁹⁄₁₆in)
	118	2	42.6cm (16¾in)
	214	2	92.1cm (36¼in)
	217	2	74.6cm (29⅜in)

Design 2

Design size
4.4 x 4cm
(1¾ x 1⁹⁄₁₆in)

Stitch count
24 x 22

Materials
See materials for
design 1

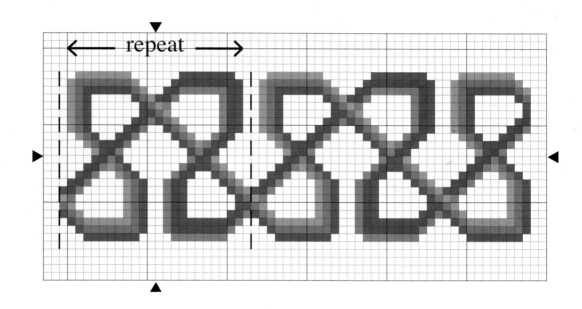

Thread required (for one repeat)

	Anchor Stranded Cotton	Strands for cross stitch	Amount
	118	2	21.3cm (8⅜in)
	217	2	21.3cm (8⅜in)
	215	2	21.8cm (8⁹⁄₁₆in)
	896	2	43.5cm (17⅛in)
	117	2	21.8cm (8⁹⁄₁₆in)

Design 3

Design size
4.7 x 4.4cm
($1^{13}/_{16}$ x $1^{3}/_{4}$in)

Stitch count
26 x 24

Materials
See materials for
design 1

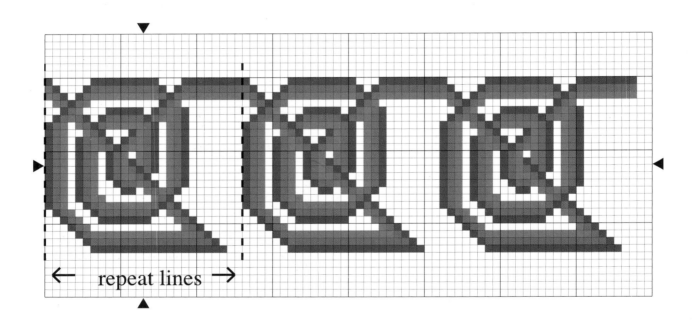

← repeat lines →

Thread required (for one repeat)

	Anchor Stranded Cotton	Strands for cross stitch	Amount
	118	2	58.8cm (23⅛in)
	215	2	49.5cm (19½in)
	896	2	63cm (24¹³⁄₁₆in)

Three Borders for a Green Bolster Cushion

These designs were worked over 2 threads on 28# Jobelan. The larger design in the centre was from a German flagon and the two smaller ones were from bronze flagons.

Design 1

Design size
7.6x 8cm
(3 x 3⅛in)

Stitch count
42 X 44

Materials
28# Jobelan

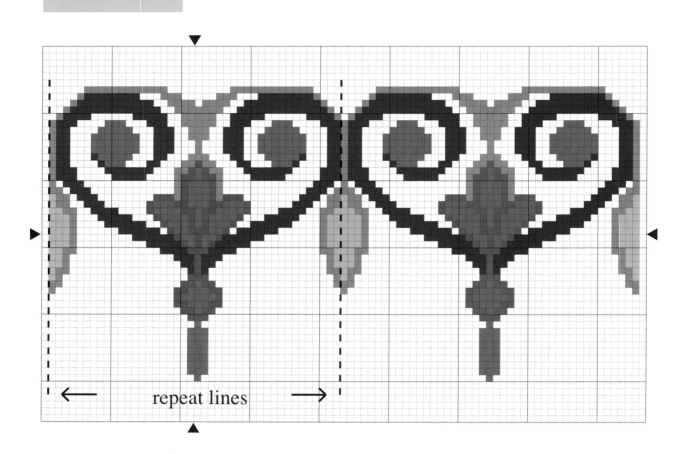

← repeat lines →

Thread required (for one repeat)

	Anchor Stranded Cotton	Strands for cross stitch	Amount
	111	2	76.4cm (30in)
	878	2	37cm (14⁹⁄₁₆in)
	70	2	138cm (54⅝in)
	68	2	46.8cm (18⅜in)
	66	2	19cm (7½in)
	215	2	19.4cm (7⅝in)

Design 2

Design size
11.6 x 4.5cm
(4⁹⁄₁₆ x 1¾in)

Stitch count
64 x 25

Materials
28# Jobelan

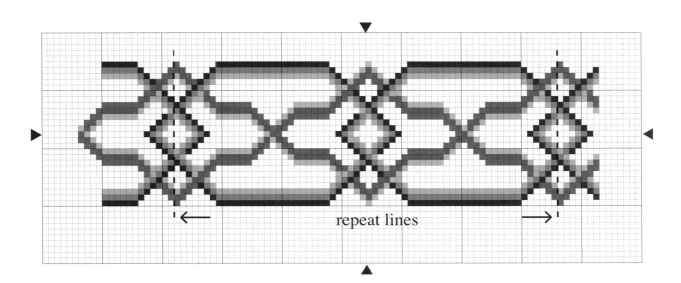

repeat lines

Thread required (for one repeat)

Anchor Stranded Cotton		Strands for cross stitch	Amount
	111	2	55.6cm (21⅞in)
	878	2	54.6cm (21½in)
	108	2	55.6cm (21⅞in)
	70	2	72.2cm (28⁷⁄₁₆in)
	68	2	68.1cm (26¹³⁄₁₆in)
	66	2	65.3cm (25¹¹⁄₁₆in)

Design 3

Design size
10.2 x 4.9cm
(4 x 1⅞in)

Stitch count
56 x 27

Materials
28# Jobelan

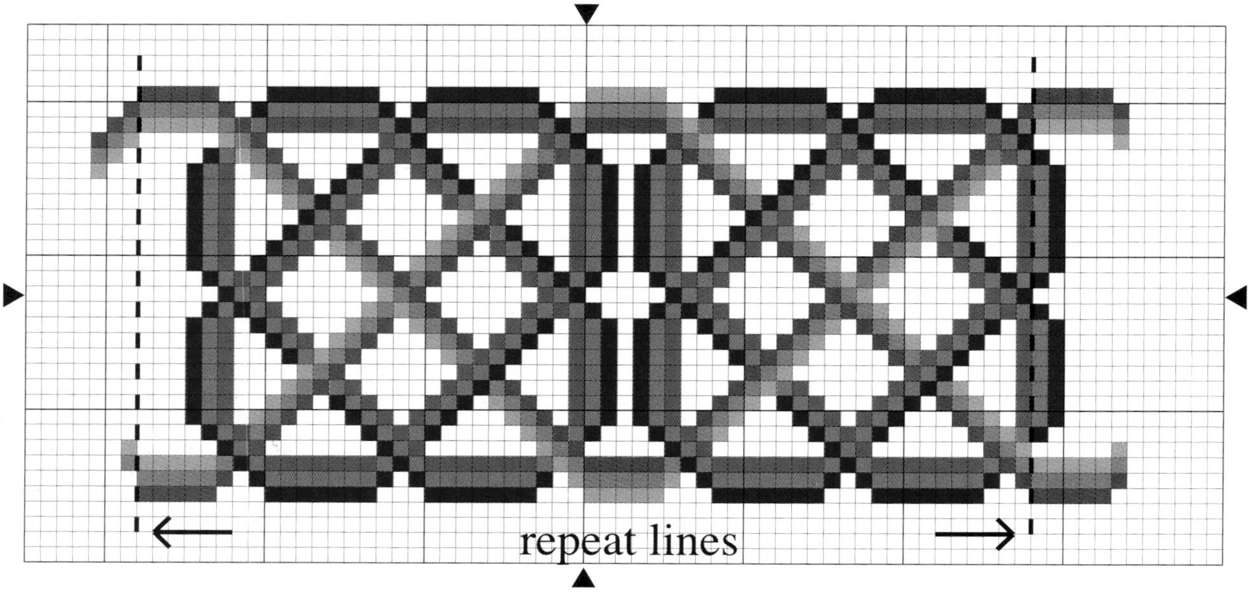

Thread required (for one repeat)

	Anchor Stranded Cotton	Strands for cross stitch	Amount
	403	2	13cm (5⅛in)
	111	2	88.9cm (35in)
	878	2	42.6cm (16¾in)
	70	2	95.4cm (37 9/16in)
	68	2	97.2cm (38¼in)
	215	2	47.2cm (18 9/16in)
	214	2	42.6cm (16¾in)

The Projects

Time for Tea

I ronically, these dainty tea time accessories were adapted from patterns on armour. The set consists of a matching tray cloth, napkin and tea cosy, all worked over 2 threads on Jobelan in pink and white stranded cotton, with small touches of blue and green.

Tray cloth

Design size
18.5 x 18.7cm
(7⁵⁄₁₆ x 7³⁄₈in)

Stitch count
102 x 102

Materials
White 28#
Jobelan,
38 x 31cm
(15 x 12³⁄₁₆in)

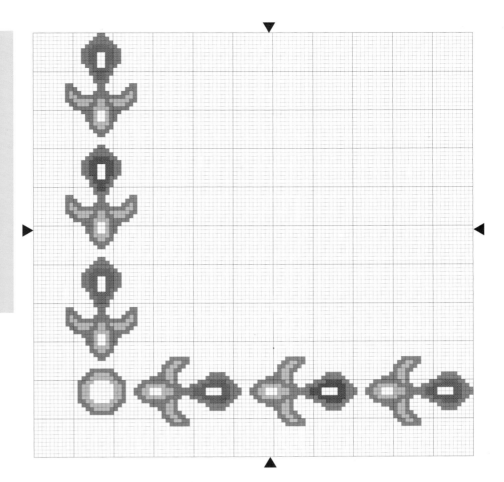

Thread required to complete all three items

	Anchor stranded cotton	Amount
	896	2 skeins
	1	1 skein
	894	1 skein
	217	1 skein
	122	1 skein

Working the design
Overcast the edges of the Jobelan to stop them fraying. Measure 5cm (2in) from the bottom and 5cm (2in) from the left-hand side. This point is the centre of the circle on the pattern. Stitch the rest of the design.

Making up
Press well on the wrong side using a damp cloth. Turn under and work a 1cm (³⁄₈in) hem all the way round.

Napkin

Design size
8.0 x 8.0cm
(3⅛ x 3⅛in)

Stitch count
44 x 44

Materials
Dusky pink 28#
Jobelan,
35 x 35cm
(13¾ x 13¾in)
1.5m (59in) fine
lace edging

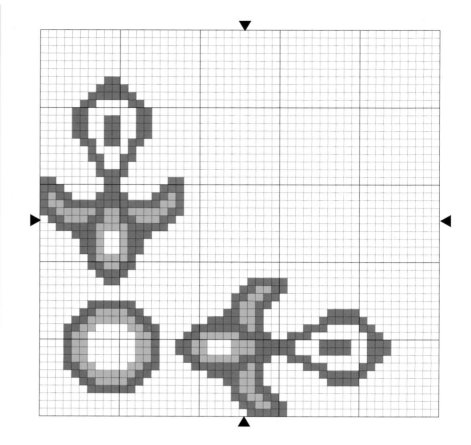

Working the design
Overcast the edges of the pink Jobelan to stop them fraying. Measure 5cm (2in) from the bottom and 5cm (2in) from the left-hand side. This point is the centre of the circle on the pattern. Stitch the rest of the design.

Making up
Press well on the wrong side using a damp cloth. Taking care to follow the threads on the Jobelan, pin and tack the lace 1cm (⅜in) from the edge on the front of the fabric. Machine this with a white, closely stitched, wide zigzag stitch. Trim the surplus fabric from the back.

Tea Cosy

Design size
29.0 x 8.7cm
(11⅜ x 3⅜in)

Stitch count
160 x 48

Materials
White 28#
Jobelan,
36 x 12cm
(14³⁄₁₆ x 4¾in)
Dusky pink 28#
Jobelan, 2 pieces
36 x 27cm
(14³⁄₁₆ x 10⅝in)
Vilene, one piece
10 x 38cm
(3¹⁵⁄₁₆ x 15in)
Heavy cotton for
lining, 2 pieces,
36 x 27cm
(14³⁄₁₆ x 10⅝in)
Two pieces
medium-weight
wadding,
35 x 23cm
(13¾ x 9in)
Tassel

Working the design
Overcast the edges of the strip of white Jobelan. Stitch the tea cosy design in the centre of the strip.

Making up
Enlarge the template so that the dimensions are 35 x 25cm (13¾ x 9¹³⁄₁₆in). Adding 3cm (1³⁄₁₆in) at the straight edge, use this template to cut two pieces of pink Jobelan and two pieces of lining. Cut two pieces of wadding the size of the template (without the 3cm/ 1³⁄₁₆in). Iron the Vilene strip on to the wrong side of the tea cosy stitching making sure it is in the centre. Fold in the long sides to make a strip, then fasten this to one piece of the tea cosy, 3cm (1³⁄₁₆in) from the bottom.

Pin and machine the pink back and front of the tea cosy right sides together, then machine the curved edge keeping 1cm (⅜in) from the edge. Trim the seam. Turn the right way out. Machine the lining pieces right sides together, then fasten the wadding to the two wrong sides of the lining. Fit the wadding and lining inside the tea cosy, wrong sides together, so that the right side of the lining forms the inside of the cosy. Turn the bottom of the pink fabric to the inside, and hem it over the edges of the wadded lining. While fastening a tassel at the top, catch in the top of the lining to prevent it moving.

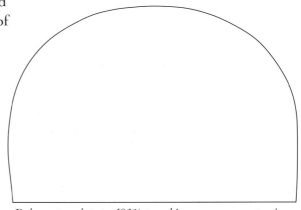

Enlarge template to 480% to achieve measurements given

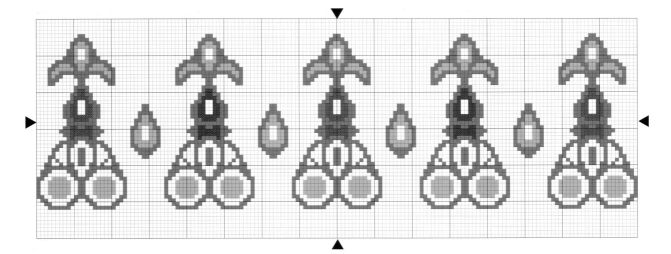

Bell Pull in Greens and Gold

This bell pull is worked mainly in shades of green and gold stranded cotton with the addition of Multi's Embellishment Yarn, which picks out the same colours. I finished it with gold cord and a chunky tassel made from the remaining threads. The design has two main sections: the top comes from a decorated letter in the *Lindisfarne Gospels* and this leads down into interwoven strands which contain small Celtic designs.

Design size

18.5 x 43.4cm
(7⁵⁄₁₆ x 17in)

Stitch count

102 x 239

Materials

14# Aida, 51 x
26cm (20 x 10¼in)
Single bell pull
end with 20cm
(7⅞in) space
1.25m (49in) of
thick gold cord
0.5m (19¹¹⁄₁₆in) of
thin gold cord
Iron-on Vilene,
one piece, 48 x
20cm (18⅞ x
7⅞in); two pieces
51 x 2.5cm
(20 x 1in); two
pieces 15 x 2.5cm
(5⅞ x 1in) and one
piece 20 x 2.5cm
(7⅞ x 1in)

A black and white version of this chart which can be enlarged on a photocopier for easier working can be found on page 181.

Thread required

	Anchor Stranded Cotton	Bond Multi	Amount
	858		2 skeins
	862		2 skeins
	403		1 skein
	1		1 skein
	306		1 skein
	860		1 skein
	861		1 skein
	307		1 skein
	859		1 skein
		Embellishment Yarn 'Woodlands'	1 reel

Working the design

Starting in the centre, stitch the design using two strands of cotton and the whole strand of Multi, working over every thread.

Making up

Press well on the wrong side, using a damp cloth. Next, prepare the Vilene. Measure 10.2cm (4in) up from the end and draw a pencil line from here to the centre bottom on each side, so you have a point. Cut this off. Place the Vilene shiny side down on the wrong side of the stitching with the point 2.5cm (1in) below the last stitch and iron in place using a dry iron (medium heat). Trim the long edges and the point to 1cm (⅜in). Turn in to the wrong side to the edges of the Vilene, and secure by ironing on the long strips of Vilene down the sides, and the two 15.3 x 2.5cm (6 x 1in) strips down the point. Turn down the top and secure with the short piece of Vilene leaving a slot opening for the bell pull rod.

Stitch the thick cord round the edges and hang a chunky tassel at the end of the point. Use the thin cord to hang the bell pull.

Zoomorphic
Bell pull

This is a large project, but as it is composed of sections it is interesting to stitch one complete animal then move on to the next. Each creature can be worked independently as a picture or card. The small individual picture shown is worked on 22# canvas using three strands, and fits an aperture of 11 x 11cm (4⁵⁄₁₆ x 4⁵⁄₁₆in). The animals were all adapted from the *Book of Kells*.
Starting at the top, the animals are an eagle (Ascension), hound, lion (Resurrection), peacock or dove, lion and calf (Death).

Design size
77.6 x 16.7cm
(30½ x 6⅝in)

Stitch count
492 x 105

Materials
16# Hardanger,
87.5 x 20cm
(34⁷⁄₁₆ x 7⅞in)
Pair of 17.8cm
(7in) bell pull ends
Iron-on Vilene: one
piece, 17 x 82.5cm
(6¹¹⁄₁₆ x 32½in); two
pieces, 4 x 82.5cm
(1½ x 32½in) and
two pieces, 4 x
17cm (1½ x 6¹¹⁄₁₆in)

Thread required

	Anchor Stranded Cotton	Strands for cross stitch	Amount
	403*	2	33.4cm (13⅛in)
	843	2	1529.9cm (602⅜in)
	890	2	1454.9cm (572¹³⁄₁₆in)
	878	2	226cm (89in)
	298*	2	794.5cm (312¹³⁄₁₆in)
	1089	2	238.5cm (93⅞in)
	846	2	3445.6cm (1356⅝in)
	878 & 1089	1 of each	664.5cm (261⅝in)
	309*	2	1228.6cm (483¹¹⁄₁₆in)
	1080	2	45.4cm (17⅞in)

(5 skeins of 846, 2 skeins of 843, 890, 309 and 1 skein of 298, 403, 878, 298, 1089 and 1080 are enough to complete the design)

Working the design
Stitch the design in the centre of the fabric using two strands of cotton.

Making up
Press the embroidery on the wrong side using a damp cloth. Carefully centre and iron the large piece of Vilene on the back of the stitched piece, lining up the threads at the sides. Trim the long edges of the Hardanger allowing 2.5cm (1in) outside the Vilene. Turn these long edges to the back of the stitching and secure with the two long narrow strips of Vilene. Fold 2.5cm (1in) to the wrong side at the top and bottom, and secure on the wrong side with the two short pieces of Vilene. Slot the bell pull ends through the top and bottom of the bell pull. Add a tassel, made from the remaining threads, at the bottom.

A Rug of Knots

This is a large project, but although it could be worked on one large piece of canvas, I think that it is far more convenient to work each individual square, then fasten them together, so I have written the instructions accordingly. If the background is light-coloured the canvas needs to be white, but if it is to be dark then brown canvas is better.

Design size
Each square on
10# canvas, 33 x
33cm (13 x 13in)

Stitch count
132 x 132

Materials
For each square:
10# canvas 41
(16in) square

Thread required
The thread key for
the rugknots can
be found on
page 53.

Thread required for one square

Anchor Tapisserie Wool: 1 skein each of the 5 shades and 1 extra skein for the colour used in the border plait; 15 skeins or 4 hanks of 8006; 3 skeins of 9800 (or 1 hank). You will need 3 skeins of black and 3 skeins of cream for the border round each square.

Working the design

Start by finding the centre of the square, then follow the centre line up. The border starts 8 squares down from the top. This leaves a bigger gap below the border of the square for the outside edge of the rug. Work the border in cross stitch. When this is complete, locate the top of the knot from the chart, and work the knot in cross stitch. The inside of the knot is black cross stitch. The cream inside gap between the knot and the border is tent stitch. When it is complete, work 1 row all the way round of tent stitch in the jade or burgundy in the border of that square. Take care to keep all tent stitches in the rug lying in the same direction.

Making up

When you have the required number of stitched squares for your rug, lay them out on the floor in the order that you choose and join the two top squares together in the following way. First, line the canvasses up, then overlap the unworked canvas by three holes and tack in place. Work tent stitch through both layers of canvas in black. There should be 3 rows of stitching. When this is complete, repeat the process with the next two squares until all the squares are stitched to a partner with the tops of the knots in the centre.

Now do the same, joining each pair until all the squares are stitched together. Turn under and tack all the way round leaving 12 holes to be worked for the edges. Now stitch these edges through both layers of canvas as before in tent stitch. Stitch 7 rows of black, then 5 outside these in cream. Oversew the side edges in cream, then tassel the ends as in the diagram. Trim off all excess canvas once the rug is complete and there is no danger of it becoming unravelled. If you wish, fasten a hessian backing on to the completed rug.

Tassels to finish off the threads

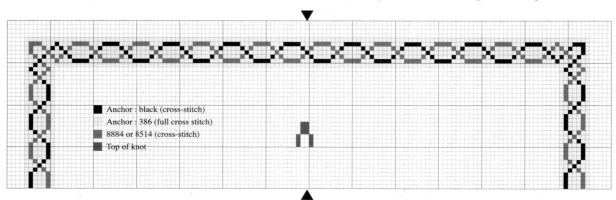

■ Anchor : black (cross-stitch)
▨ Anchor : 386 (full cross stitch)
▨ 8884 or 8514 (cross-stitch)
▨ Top of knot

Knot 1

Design size
26.9 x 23.1cm
(10⅚ x 9⅟₆in)

Stitch count
106 x 91

Materials
10# fabric

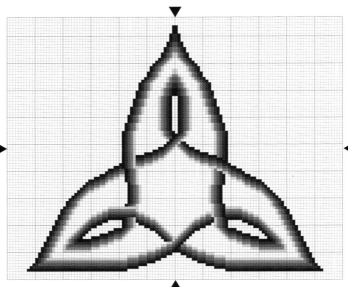

Knot 2

Design size
26.2 x 23.1cm
(10⅚ x 9⅟₆in)

Stitch count
103 x 91

Materials
10# fabric

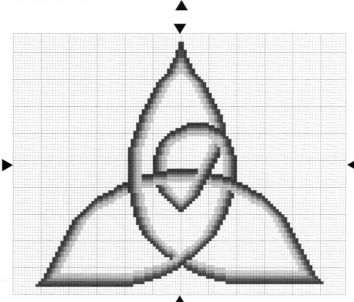

Knot 3

Design size
26.7 x 23.1cm
(10½ X 9⅟₆in)

Stitch count
105 x 91

Materials
10# fabric

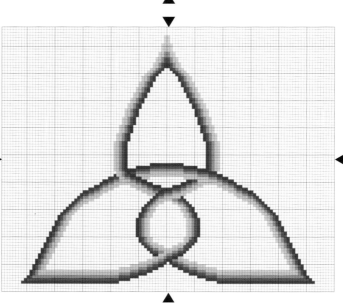

Knot 4

Design size
26.7 x 23.1cm
(10½ x 9⅒in)

Stitch count
105 x 91

Materials
10# fabric

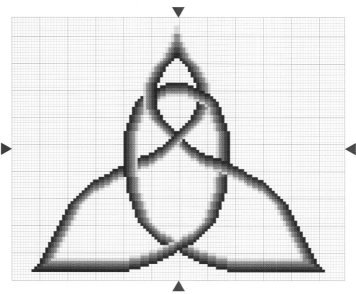

Knot 5

Design size
26.7 x 23.1cm
(10½ x 9⅒in)

Stitch count
105 x 91

Materials
10# fabric

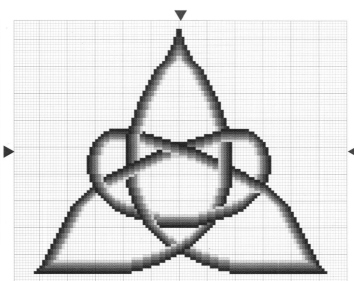

Knot 6

Design size
26.7 x 23.9cm
(10½ x 9⅜in)

Stitch count
105 x 94

Materials
10# fabric

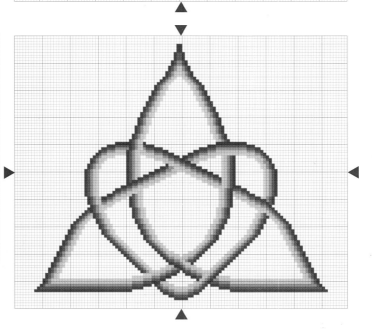

Pins and Needles

For these designs I used variations on an interwoven plait design. The colour combination with the shiny beads to give it a highlight works really well, although I was originally going to use all shades of blue. The basic pattern could easily be adapted or extended for lots of purposes.

Pincushion

Design size
12.3 x 12.2cm
($4^{13}/_{16}$ x $4^{13}/_{16}$in)

Materials
28# Jobelan,
21 x 21cm
(8¼ x 8¼in)
2.5cm (1in) square
of iron-on Vilene
40 x Mill Hill
beads, no 03035

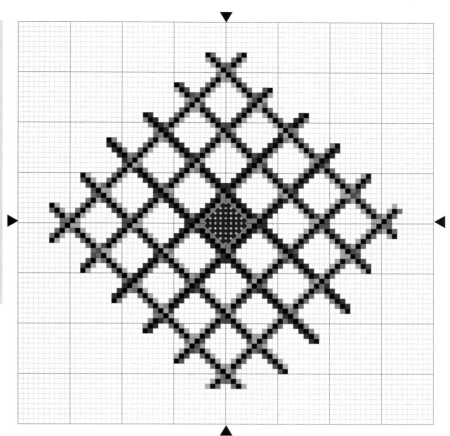

Threads required (for all three items)

	Anchor Stranded Cotton	Amount
■	403	1 skein
■	189	1 skein
■	186	1 skein
■	66	1 skein
■	69	1 skein
■	1068	1 skein
■	1062	1 skein

Working the design
Overcast the edges of the Jobelan to prevent fraying. Work the pincushion in the centre of the fabric over 2 threads using 2 strands. Iron the Vilene on the back of the centre square to strengthen the fabric, then add the beads using 1 strand of the cotton.

Making up
Stretch the stitching tightly over the base interior and fasten either by stapling or gluing underneath. Screw the cushion back into the base.

Needlecase

Design size
8.3 x 8.3cm
(3¼ x 3¼in)

Materials
28# Jobelan,
20 x 14cm
(7⅞ x 5½in)
Iron-on Vilene,
19 x 9cm
(7½ x 3½in)
Cotton lining,
21 x 11cm
(8¼ x 4⁵⁄₁₆in)
Two pieces of felt,
16 x 8cm
(6⁵⁄₁₆ x 3⅛in)
40 x Mill Hill
beads 03035

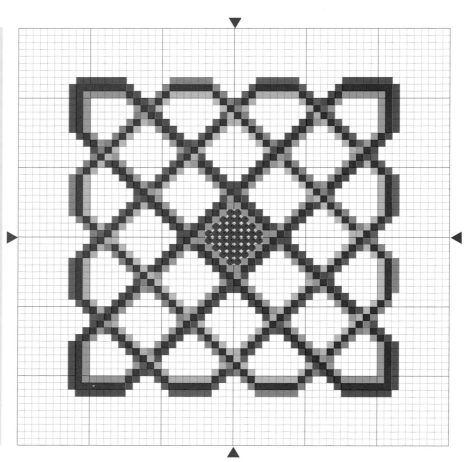

Working the design
Fold the needlecase fabric to find the centre line of the length,
then work the embroidery 1cm (⅜in) to the right of the centre.
Iron the Vilene on to the centre of the fabric at the back. Stitch on
the beads in the centre using 1 strand of the cotton.

Making up
Trim to 1cm (⅜in) round the edge of the Vilene. Turn in 1cm (⅜in)
on the lining then slip-stitch to the Jobelan. Pink the edges of the
felt then stitch them in the centre of the case with back-stitch.
Make a twisted cord from the remaining threads. Stitch it down
the spine and the inside crease, then make the ends into a tassel.

Needle cushion

Design size
3.9 x 3.9cm
(1½ x 1½in)

Materials
22# canvas, two
pieces 6 x 6cm
(2⅜ x 2⅜in)
Small amount of
filling
Wooden beads

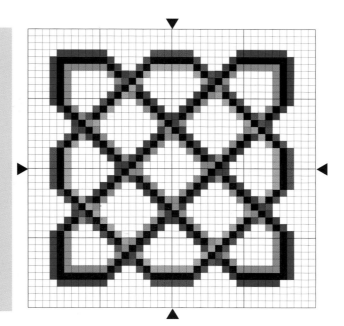

Working the design
Use 3 strands of cotton and half cross stitch to work the design for
the needle cushion in the centre of both of the pieces of canvas.
Work 1 row of white all the way round and fill the design spaces
in white.

Making up
Trim the edges carefully to leave 4 threads of canvas at each side.
Slightly mitre the corners. With wrong sides facing, oversew the
two pieces together across the canvas in 6 strands of 69 to make an
edge. Just before completing the fourth side, tuck a little filling in,
then finish off. Thread beads on to one corner and attach a tassel
made from remaining threads.

Scented Wardrobe Hanger

This is a practical and pretty item to stitch and is especially useful as a present for those annoying people who seem to have everything. The spiral designs are from Celtic stonework. I have included two colours from Bond Multi's Embellishment yarn, but one reel would be sufficient for both designs if you wanted to do them the same colour.

Design size
9.5 x 9.5cm
(3¾ x 3¾in)

Stitch count
60 x 60

Materials
16# Hardanger,
12 x 12cm
(4¾ x 4¾in)
Iron-on Vilene,
12cm (4¾in)
square
Gathered lace,
45cm (17¹¹⁄₁₆in)
Pretty cotton
backing, 2 x 15cm
(5⅞in) squares
Strip of backing
for frill, 8 x 60cm
(3⅛ x 23⅝in)
Piece of cord or
ribbon, 45cm
(18in)
Padded coat
hanger
Small amount of
potpourri or filling
scented with oil

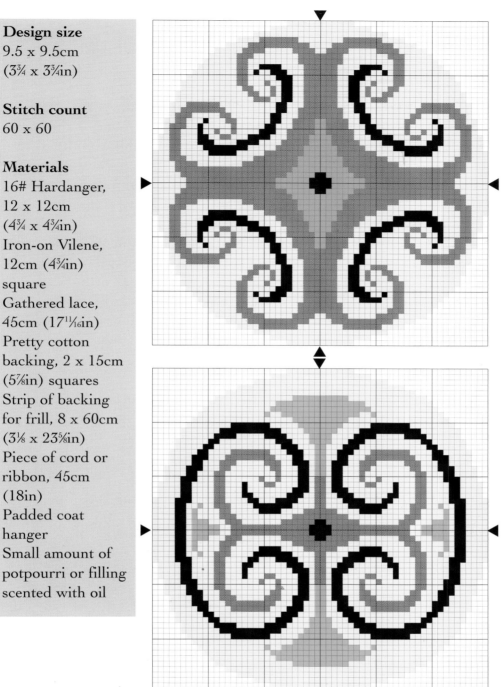

Threads required

	Anchor Stranded Cotton	Amount (design 1)	Amount (design 2)
	386	2 skeins	2 skeins
	152	1 skein	1 skein
	970	1 skein	1 skein
	Bond Multi's Embellishment	(Caribe) 1 reel	(Tapestry) 1 reel

Working the design

Overcast the Hardanger to prevent fraying. Stitch the design in the centre using 2 strands cotton and 1 strand of Multi's.

Making up

Press the embroidery on the wrong side on a padded board. Iron the Vilene on the back with the design in the centre. On the back, in pencil, draw a circle with a 10cm (4in) diameter, then carefully cut it out. Tack this in the centre of one of the backing pieces with the wrong side of the stitching to the right side of the backing. Tack the lace round to cover the edge of the circle, then stitch round the edge of the lace with a zigzag stitch to secure the Hardanger and the lace.

Fold the frill strip in half lengthways, then gather it and tack it to the right side of the backing (the one with the embroidery fastened to it) facing in, with the two raw edges together on the outside. Place the second backing piece face down, then stitch the two pieces together 1cm (⅜in) out from the lace, to form an inside-out bag. Leave 4cm (1.5in) opening to allow the bag to be turned right way out. Turn through to the right side, fill the bag and slip-stitch the opening. At the same time, insert one of the ends of the ribbon into the opening and secure it as you stitch.

Repeat this whole process with the other bag, but when fastening the opening, insert the remaining end of the ribbon and secure. Twist the ribbon round the coat hanger hook, then this can be hung among your clothes to keep them delicately perfumed.

Rocking Chair Accessories

This can give a whole new look to an old rocking chair. The designs came from patterns inside illuminated letters in the *Book of Kells* and a carpet page from the *Book of Durrow*. I chose to stitch it in shades of pink and green to match my bedroom, but you could match the colours to the room in which you keep your chair. The set would look equally good on a wooden or white chair. The instructions for the seat are given for the centre pattern only, as the outside stitching needs to fit your own chair. If you are not lucky enough to have a rocking chair, these designs would make lovely dining-chair cushions. I found the shaped cushion on a garden chair and re-covered it with tapestry. Draw round the cushion on to the canvas, allowing 5cm (2in) all the way round, then cut it out.

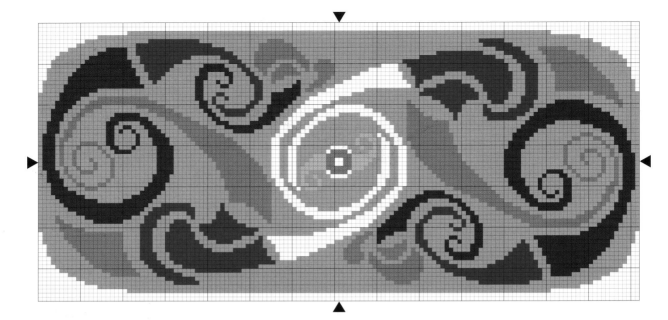

Header cushion

Design size
On 10# canvas,
36.1 x 16.3cm
(14³⁄₁₆ x 6³⁄₈in)

Stitch count
142 x 64

Materials
10# canvas,
40 x 20cm (15¾
x 7⅞in)
Backing fabric,
40 x 20cm
(15¾ x 7⅞in)
Two strips backing
fabric, 1m x 7cm
(39⅜ x 2¾in) or
1m (39⅜in) ribbon
Polyester filling

Thread required

	Anchor Tapisserie Wool	Amount
	9074	6 skeins
	9080	2 skeins
	8400	2 skeins
	8404	2 skeins
	8398	1 skein
	8000	1 skein

Working the design
Stitch the header cushion design in the centre of the fabric in tent stitch.

Making up
First, make four ties by cutting each long strip of backing fabric in half, then stitch the right sides of each piece together down the long edges. Turn the right way out, tuck in the ends and oversew. Next, place the right side of the stitching to the right side of the backing. Insert the four ties so that they are 10cm (4in) in from each end at the top and the bottom. Allow approximately 1cm (⅜in) to be inside the cushion when it is turned right way out. Stitch the two pieces of the cushion together, remembering to leave a 12.5cm (4⅞in) gap to allow the cushion to be turned. Turn the cushion the right way out, stuff firmly, then carefully slip-stitch the opening closed.

Seat cushion

Design size
On 12# canvas,
28.6 x 28.2cm
(11¼ x 11⅛in)

Stitch count
135 x 133

Materials
12# canvas to fit
your chair (add
5cm/2in allowance
all the way round)
Backing fabric to
match the canvas
size
Two strips backing
fabric, 1m x 7cm
(39⅜ x 2¾in) or
1m (39⅜in) ribbon
Cushion interior

There is a black and white version of this chart, which can be enlarged, on page 183.

Thread required

	Anchor Tapisserie Wool	Amount
	9074 (for the background)	
	8000	5 skeins
	9080	3 skeins
	8404	3 skeins
	8398	2 skeins
	9078	1 skein
	8400	1 skein

Working the design
When you have cut out the canvas following the above instructions, stitch the design in the centre, using tent stitch.

Making up
Make two long ties and insert them into the back of the cushion 8cm (3⅛in) in from the side edges. Place the stitching and backing right sides together and stitch, remembering to leave a 12.5cm (4⅞in) gap at the back. Turn the right way out, then insert the cushion pad and slip-stitch closed.

Scatter cushion

Design size
On 14# Jobelan over 2 threads, 23.8 x 23.2cm (9⅜ x 9⅛in)

Stitch count
131 x 128

Materials
28# white Jobelan, 32cm (12⁹⁄₁₆in) square Backing fabric, 42cm x 42cm (16½ x 16½in) and 4 strips each 42 x 10cm (16½ x 4in) 41cm (16⅛in) cushion pad

There is a black and white version of this chart, which can be enlarged, on page 184.

Thread required

Anchor Stranded Cotton

3 skeins x 217
2 skeins x 215, 895, 897
1 skein x 1 and 896

Working the design
Overcast the edges of the Jobelan to prevent fraying, then stitch the design in the centre using 2 strands in cross stitch.

Making up
On each of the strips press under a 2cm (¾in) turn on one long side. Measure and tack a line on the embroidered front 5cm (2in) from the stitching. Then starting at the top edge, lay one of the folded strips along the tacked line and machine close to the fold. Repeat down one side, then across the bottom and the other side, so that the strips form a border round the stitched centre right sides together, stitch the embroidery to the backing (allow a 1cm (⅜in) seam allowance) leaving a gap to enable the cover to be turned right way out. Turn it the right way out, insert the cushion pad and slip-stitch closed.

Desk Set

This cheerful set would enhance any desk. It consists of a matching noteblock holder, storage pot for pencils and telephone or address book. Both the noteblock holder and the pencil pot have two knot designs and a small design with an initial. More letters and alphabets can be found in the Illuminated Letters section which begins on page 97.

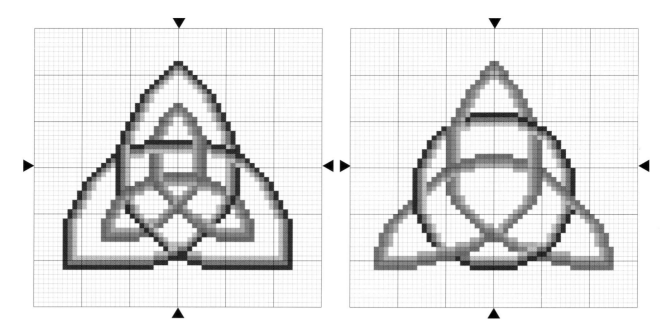

Noteblock holder

Design size
On 14# Aida,
8.7 x 8.2cm
(3⅜ x 3³⁄₁₆in)

Stitch count
48 x 45

Materials
14# Aida, 3 pieces,
12 x 11cm
(4¹¹⁄₁₆ x 4⁵⁄₁₆in)
Iron-on Vilene, 3
pieces, 9.75 x 9cm
(3¹³⁄₁₆ x 3½in)
Noteblock holder

Threads required (for all three items)

	Anchor Stranded Cotton	Amount
	204	1 skein
	230	1 skein
	236	1 skein
	235	1 skein
	232	1 skein
	335	1 skein
	1042	1 skein
	332	1 skein
	329	1 skein

Working the design

Note that the width is wider than the length, so the designs are landscape, not portrait. Stitch all three designs in cross stitch using 2 threads.

Stitch the 3 designs for the noteblock holder in the centre of the14# Aida.

Making up

For the noteblock holder and pencil pot, iron the pieces of Vilene carefully on the centre back of the embroidery. Remember the designs are not as tall as they are wide. Cut out the piece of stitching backed by the Vilene and slide it into the plastic sleeve provided with the pots.

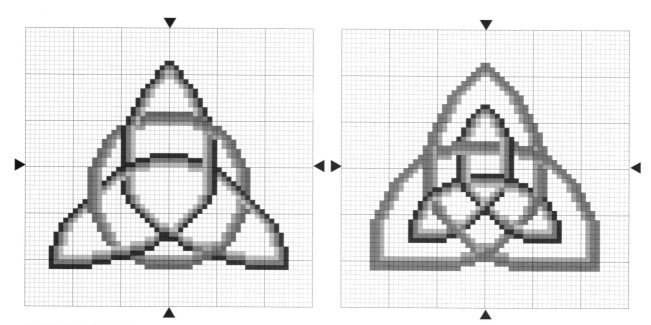

Pencil pot

Design size
On 18# Aida,
6.8 x 6.4cm
($2^{11}/_{16}$ x $2^{1}/_{2}$in)

Stitch count
48 x 45

Materials
18# Aida, 3 pieces,
10 x 10.5cm
($3^{7}/_{8}$ x $4^{1}/_{8}$in)
Iron on Vilene, 3
pieces, 8 x 8.5cm
($3^{1}/_{8}$ x $3^{5}/_{16}$in)
Pencil pot

Making up
See under Noteblock holder.

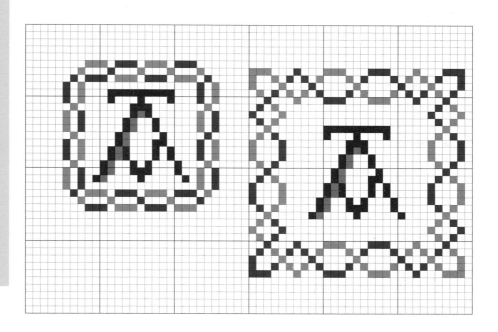

Telephone book

Design size
On 19# Easistitch,
12 x 12cm
(4^{11}⁄₁₆ x 4^{11}⁄₁₆in)

Stitch count
90 x 90

Materials
Telephone book
of your choice
19# Easistitch.
Measure the book
open flat, adding
5cm (2in) for each
side and 2cm (¾in)
at both the top
and the bottom.
This is the size
you will need.
Iron-on Vilene.
This needs to be
the size of the
open book without
any turnings. Also,
cut two pieces
2.5cm (1in) wide
and the length of
the book.
Cord to fit all the
way round the
outside of the
book plus three
times the height.

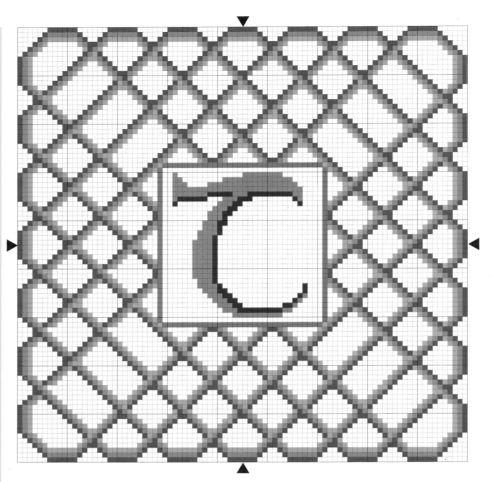

Working the design
Overcast the Easistitch to prevent fraying. Wrap the Easistitch
round the book, then locate the stitching so that it is positioned in
the centre of the front.

Making up
Iron on the Vilene so that it is in the centre. Turn in the top and
bottom to the height of the book and secure with the strips of
Vilene. Turn in and stitch the side flaps to make an envelope
pocket for the book to slide into.

The cord needs to be threaded up the spine leaving 10cm
(3⅞in) below, then stitched all the way round the edge and finally
taken down the outside of the spine. Wrap the two ends together
with a length of 335 and unravel the ends of the cord to make a
sort of tassel.

footstool

The centre of this design was an adaptation of a palmette design found on a torque. The border came partly from a decorated letter. The colours are striking with the contrasting white and dark blue. All of the amounts are given for the centre design only, because the dark blue border will need to be extended or contracted to fit your stool.

There is a black and white version of this chart, which can be enlarged, on page 185.

Design size
Centre on 14#
canvas:
33.2 x 20.5cm
(13 x 8in)

Stitch count
Centre: 183 x 113

Materials
Footstool
White 14# canvas,
large enough to fit
your stool

Threads required

	Anchor Tapisserie Wool	Amount
	8740 (for the border)	(variable)
	8740	1 hank
	8000	10 skeins
	8920	2 skeins
	8712	1 skein
	8820	1 skein
	8794	1 skein
	8970	1 skein
	8822	1 skein

Working the design
Stitch the design in the centre of the canvas using tent stitch.
Remember to fill in the spaces in the design with 8000 (white).
This is not on the chart, because it makes the chart clearer for you
to follow.

Making up
Take out the cushion seat from the stool then stretch the canvas
across the top and fasten either by lacing or by stapling on the
underneath. Replace the cushion pad into the stool.

Door Decorations

This set of a doorstop brick and complementary fingerplate would liven up any door. Make it in colours to match your room, or in bright colours like these. The fingerplate design came from a scabbard and I developed the idea for the doorbrick by adding some knot designs.

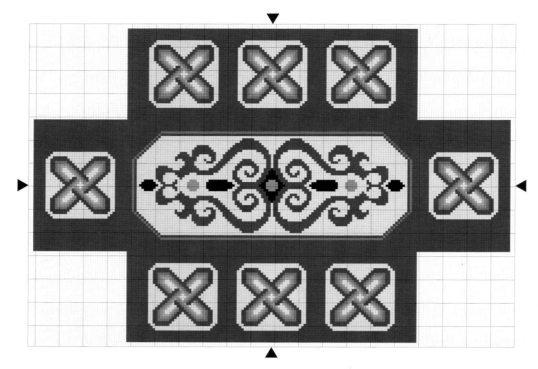

There is a black and white version of this chart, which can be enlarged, on page 186.

Doorstop brick

Design size
14# canvas:
36.1 x 24.5cm
(14¼ x 9½in)

Stitch count
Doorstop brick:
195 x 135

Materials
14# canvas:
39 x 27cm
(15½ x 10½in)
Piece firm felt:
11 x 22.5cm
(4½ x 8¾in)
Iron-on Vilene:
11 x 22.5cm
(4⅓ x 8¾in)
1 brick, approx.
22 x 10.5 x 7cm
(8½ x 4 x 2¾in)
Wadding

Thread required

	Anchor Tapisserie Wool	Amount
	9646	10 skeins
	8006	6 skeins
	9800	1 skein
	8236	1 skein
	8198	1 skein
	8168	1 skein

Working the design
Stitch the design in the centre of the canvas in tent stitch.

Making up
When it is complete, with right sides of the work together, join A to A and stitch up the side, B to B etc. When you turn it the right way out, you will have a brick shape. Fit it over the brick, wrapping wadding round the brick to give a close fit. Lace the edges together across the bottom of the brick. Iron the Vilene on to the back of the felt. Slip-stitch the felt to the canvas bottom of the brick to finish.

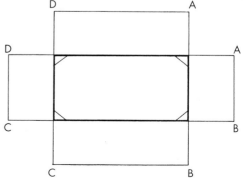

Fingerplate

Design size
24.7 x 4.7cm
(9¾ x 1⅞in)

Stitch count
136 x 26

Materials
14# 55mm Aida
cream band,
1 piece 25cm
(9¾in) long
Iron-on Vilene,
5 x 25cm
(2 x 9¾in)
Anchor Stranded
Cotton as follows:
1 skein x 403,
1088, 341, 335,
330, 386
1 doorplate from
Framecraft
Miniatures

Thread required

■	403
■	1088
■	341
■	335
■	330
	386

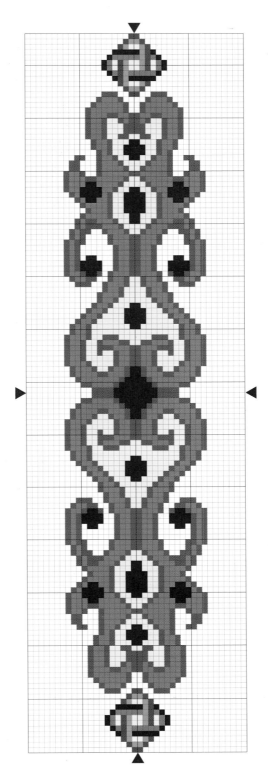

Working the design
Work the design in cross stitch in the centre of the band using
2 strands.

Making up
Iron the Vilene on to the centre back. Insert into the fingerplate
and stick on the backing that comes with it.

Charts for Enlarging

These black and white charts of the larger designs in this book can be enlarged on a photocopier to make them easier to work

The image legend reads:

Symbol	Description
■	Anchor 403
→	Anchor 1
H	Anchor 858
W	Multi's Embellishment Yarn
○	Anchor 862
⊠	Anchor 306
▼	Anchor 860
＼	Anchor 861
∪	Anchor 307
▨	Anchor 859
—	Anchor 403 (backstitch)

*Bell Pull in
Greens and Gold
(see page 150)*

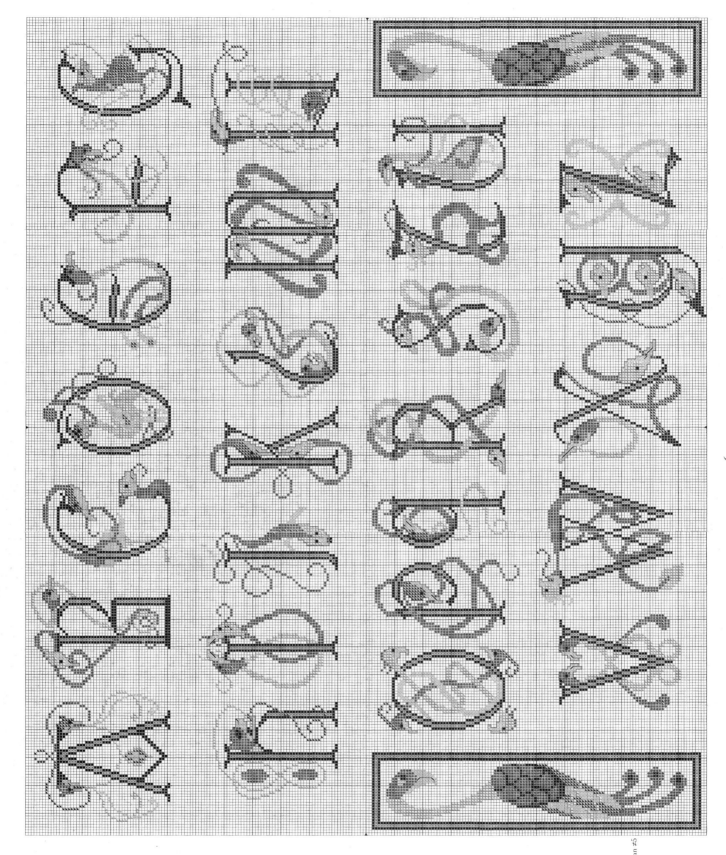

Anchor 403
Anchor 1
Anchor 266
Anchor 298
Kreinik Japan #5
Anchor 46
Anchor 340
Anchor 405 (backstitch)

⊞ Anchor 9080	■ Anchor 8400
⊖ Anchor 9078	▩ Anchor 8404
☐ Anchor 9074 (surround)	⊡ Anchor 8000
● Anchor 8398	

Seat Cushion (see page 167)

■	Anchor 217	●	Anchor 895
⊖	Anchor 215	◢	Anchor 896
·	Anchor 1	⋃	Anchor 897

Scatter Cushion (see page 167)

Footstool (see page 175)

Anchor 9800
Anchor 9646
Anchor 8236
Anchor 8198
Anchor 8168
Anchor 8006

Doorstop Brick (see page 177)

Thread Conversion Chart

Anchor	DMC	Madeira	Anchor	DMC	Madeira	Anchor	DMC	Madeira
1	B5200	2401	266	470/3347	1502	905	3021/3031	1904
8	353/3824	0304	268	937/3345	1504	968	778	0808
9	352	0303	281	581/731/732	1612	1002	977	2301
10	35	0406	298	972	0107	1013	356/3778	2310
11	350	0213	306	3820	2514	1021	761	0404
13	349/817	0211	307	783	2514	1022	760	0404
19	304	0407	308	781/782	2211	1023	3712	0405
44	815	0513	309	780	2213	1024	3328	0406
45	814	2606	323	722/3825	0307	1025	347	0407
46	666	0210	324	721	0308	1027	3722	0812
47	321	0510	326	20	0309	1028	3685	2608
68	3687	0604	330	608/947	0205	1031	3753	1001
69	3803	2609	333	900	0206	1033	932	1710
76	3731/961	0505	334	606	0209	1034	931	1711
108	210	2711	340	919	0313	1036	3750	1712
109	209	2711	341	918	0314			
110	208	2710	351	400	2304			
117	341	0901	352	300	2304			
118	340	0902	358	433	2008			
119	333	0903	380	898	2005			
120	3747	0909	397	3072	1901			
132	797	0912	398	415	1802			
133	796	0913	400	317	1714			
185	964	1112	401	535	1713			
186	959	1113	403	310	2400			
187	958	1114	778	3774	2309			
188	3812	2706	875	3813/3817	1702			
204	913	1212	876	503/3816	1703			
205	911	1213	877	502/3817	1205			
206	504/564	1210	878	501	1205			
208	563	1207	890	729	2209			
209	912	1213	891	676	2208			
235	318/414	1801	893	224	0404			
236	413/3799	1713	895	223	0812			
244	987	1305	896	3721	0810			
264	3348	1409	897	221/902	2606			
265	471	1308	899	3023	1906			

Note

DMC and Madeira threads equivalents given are the closest colour matches to the Anchor range; in some instances they may not be exactly the same.

TITLES AVAILABLE FROM
GMC Publications

BOOKS

UPHOLSTERY

The Upholsterer's Pocket Reference Book	*David James*
Upholstery: A Complete Course (Revised Edition)	*David James*
Upholstery Restoration	*David James*
Upholstery Techniques & Projects	*David James*
Upholstery Tips and Hints	*David James*

DOLLS' HOUSES AND MINIATURES

Architecture for Dolls' Houses	*Joyce Percival*
A Beginners' Guide to the Dolls' House Hobby	*Jean Nisbett*
Celtic, Medieval and Tudor Wall Hangings in 1/12 Scale Needlepoint	
	Sandra Whitehead
The Complete Dolls' House Book	*Jean Nisbett*
The Dolls' House 1/24 Scale: A Complete Introduction	*Jean Nisbett*
Dolls' House Accessories, Fixtures and Fittings	*Andrea Barham*
Dolls' House Bathrooms: Lots of Little Loos	*Patricia King*
Dolls' House Fireplaces and Stoves	*Patricia King*
Easy to Make Dolls' House Accessories	*Andrea Barham*
Heraldic Miniature Knights	*Peter Greenhill*
How to Make Your Dolls' House Special: Fresh Ideas for Decorating	
	Beryl Armstrong
Make Your Own Dolls' House Furniture	*Maurice Harper*
Making Dolls' House Furniture	*Patricia King*
Making Georgian Dolls' Houses	*Derek Rowbottom*
Making Miniature Gardens	*Freida Gray*
Making Miniature Oriental Rugs & Carpets	*Meik & Ian McNaughton*
Making Period Dolls' House Accessories	*Andrea Barham*
Making 1/12 Scale Character Figures	*James Carrington*
Making Tudor Dolls' Houses	*Derek Rowbottom*
Making Victorian Dolls' House Furniture	*Patricia King*
Miniature Bobbin Lace	*Roz Snowden*
Miniature Embroidery for the Georgian Dolls' House	*Pamela Warner*
Miniature Embroidery for the Victorian Dolls' House	*Pamela Warner*
Miniature Needlepoint Carpets	*Janet Granger*
More Miniature Oriental Rugs & Carpets	*Meik & Ian McNaughton*
Needlepoint 1/12 Scale: Design Collections for the Dolls' House	
	Felicity Price
The Secrets of the Dolls' House Makers	*Jean Nisbett*

CRAFTS

American Patchwork Designs in Needlepoint	*Melanie Tacon*
A Beginners' Guide to Rubber Stamping	*Brenda Hunt*
Blackwork: A New Approach	*Brenda Day*
Celtic Cross Stitch Designs	*Carol Phillipson*
Celtic Knotwork Designs	*Sheila Sturrock*
Celtic Knotwork Handbook	*Sheila Sturrock*
Celtic Spirals and Other Designs	*Sheila Sturrock*
Collage from Seeds, Leaves and Flowers	*Joan Carver*
Complete Pyrography	*Stephen Poole*
Contemporary Smocking	*Dorothea Hall*
Creating Colour with Dylon	*Dylon International*
Creative Doughcraft	*Patricia Hughes*
Creative Embroidery Techniques Using Colour Through Gold	
	Daphne J. Ashby & Jackie Woolsey
The Creative Quilter: Techniques and Projects	*Pauline Brown*
Decorative Beaded Purses	*Enid Taylor*
Designing and Making Cards	*Glennis Gilruth*
Glass Engraving Pattern Book	*John Everett*
Glass Painting	*Emma Sedman*
How to Arrange Flowers: A Japanese Approach to English Design	
	Taeko Marvelly
An Introduction to Crewel Embroidery	*Mave Glenny*
Making and Using Working Drawings for Realistic Model Animals	
	Basil F. Fordham
Making Character Bears	*Valerie Tyler*
Making Decorative Screens	*Amanda Howes*
Making Fairies and Fantastical Creatures	*Julie Sharp*

Making Greetings Cards for Beginners	*Pat Sutherland*
Making Hand-Sewn Boxes: Techniques and Projects	*Jackie Woolsey*
Making Knitwear Fit	*Pat Ashforth & Steve Plummer*
Making Mini Cards, Gift Tags & Invitations	*Glennis Gilruth*
Making Soft-Bodied Dough Characters	*Patricia Hughes*
Natural Ideas for Christmas: Fantastic Decorations to Make	
	Josie Cameron-Ashcroft & Carol Cox
Needlepoint: A Foundation Course	*Sandra Hardy*
Patchwork for Beginners	*Pauline Brown*
Pyrography Designs	*Norma Gregory*
Pyrography Handbook (Practical Crafts)	*Stephen Poole*
Ribbons and Roses	*Lee Lockheed*
Rose Windows for Quilters	*Angela Besley*
Rubber Stamping with Other Crafts	*Lynne Garner*
Sponge Painting	*Ann Rooney*
Step-by-Step Pyrography Projects for the Solid Point Machine	
	Norma Gregory
Tassel Making for Beginners	*Enid Taylor*
Tatting Collage	*Lindsay Rogers*
Temari: A Traditional Japanese Embroidery Technique	*Margaret Ludlow*
Theatre Models in Paper and Card	*Robert Burgess*
Wool Embroidery and Design	*Lee Lockheed*

VIDEOS

Drop-in and Pinstuffed Seats	*David James*
Stuffover Upholstery	*David James*
Elliptical Turning	*David Springett*
Woodturning Wizardry	*David Springett*
Turning Between Centres: The Basics	*Dennis White*
Turning Bowls	*Dennis White*
Boxes, Goblets and Screw Threads	*Dennis White*
Novelties and Projects	*Dennis White*
Classic Profiles	*Dennis White*
Twists and Advanced Turning	*Dennis White*
Sharpening the Professional Way	*Jim Kingshott*
Sharpening Turning & Carving Tools	*Jim Kingshott*
Bowl Turning	*John Jordan*
Hollow Turning	*John Jordan*
Woodturning: A Foundation Course	*Keith Rowley*
Carving a Figure: The Female Form	*Ray Gonzalez*
The Router: A Beginner's Guide	*Alan Goodsell*
The Scroll Saw: A Beginner's Guide	*John Burke*

MAGAZINES

WOODTURNING ◆ WOODCARVING
THE ROUTER ◆ FURNITURE & CABINETMAKING
WOODWORKING ◆ THE DOLLS' HOUSE
MAGAZINE ◆ WATER GARDENING
EXOTIC GARDENING ◆ GARDEN CALENDAR
OUTDOOR PHOTOGRAPHY ◆ BUSINESSMATTERS

The above represents a selection of titles currently published or scheduled to be published.

All are available direct from the Publishers or through bookshops, newsagents and specialist retailers.

To place an order, or to obtain a complete catalogue, contact:

GMC Publications,
Castle Place, 166 High Street, Lewes, East Sussex
BN7 1XU, United Kingdom
Tel: 01273 488005 Fax: 01273 478606

Orders by credit card are accepted